How to Paint A Still Life In Watercolor

Cherries and Glass

by Debbie Waldorf Johnson

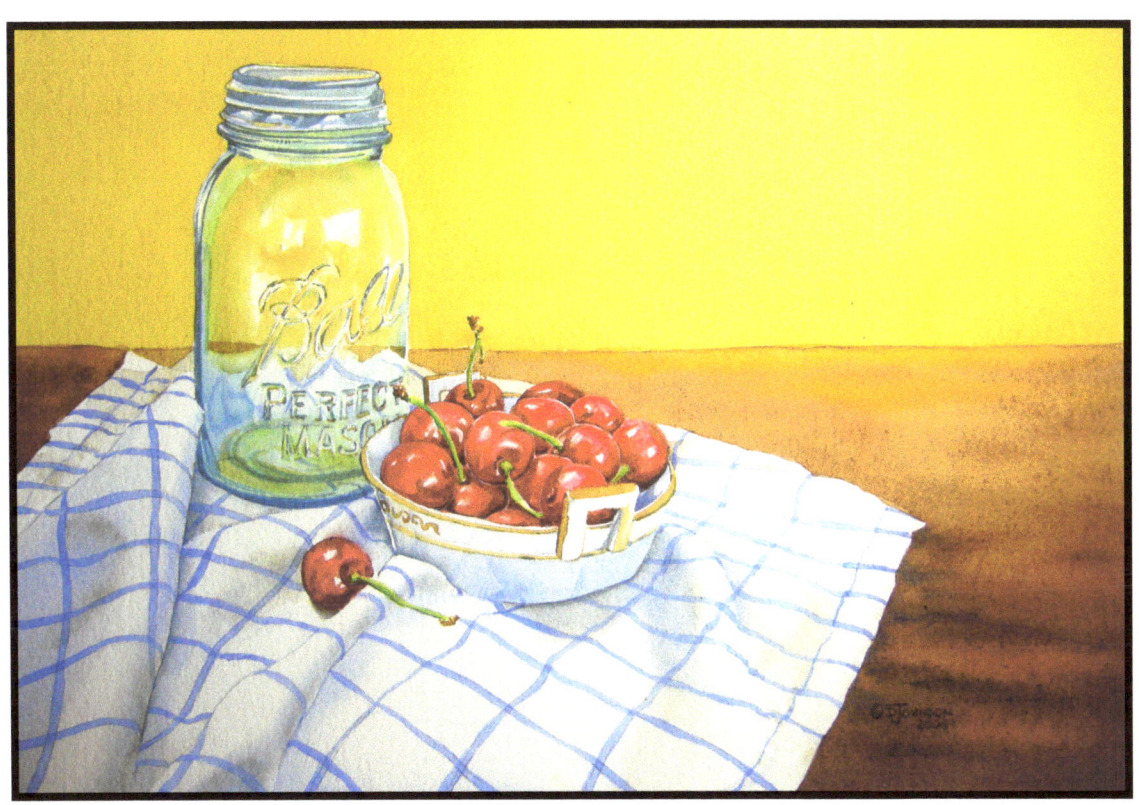

Table of Contents

Review of Basic Painting Skills

Before working on a painting, review some of the basic skills required in watercolor painting.

When preparing for a wash (application of paint in a watercolor painting) always begin with a big puddle of wet paint in your palette.

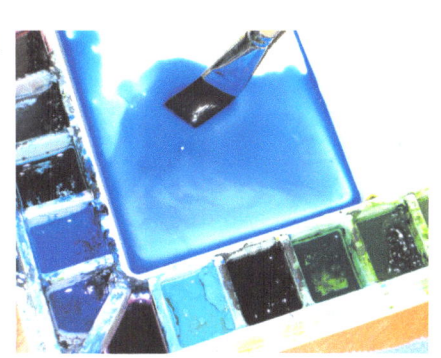

Draw four loose rectangles on a piece of watercolor paper. Each rectangle should be about four by five inches, approximately. Draw these loosely; there is no need to use a ruler!

Flat Wash - An even distribution of color in a small or large area. This is the foundational wash for all other washes used in watercolor painting.

Hold your paper in your non-painting hand at a slight angle, about 25 - 35 degrees. Start at the high end so that your paint will float toward the next stroke. Using a 1 inch flat wash brush, draw a wet line of paint from one edge of the rectangle to another. The paint should be wet enough to leave a bead or puddle of wet paint along the edge of your mark but not so much that the bead of paint drips beyond your stroke.

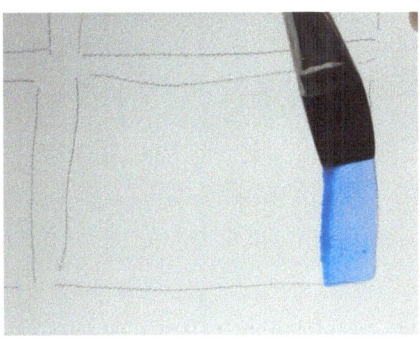

Reload your brush quickly. As you pull the next stroke, again with very wet paint, be sure it touches the puddle or bead of paint from the previous stroke. This pulls the wetness into the next stroke. Continue holding the paper at a slight angle to keep the bead at the same edge of the stroke so that you can touch it again when making the next stroke.

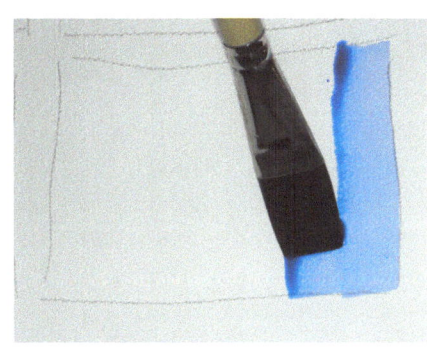

When you completely fill the rectangle, touch your brush on a paper towel, or an old wash cloth, and use the relatively dried brush to syphon the last bead of paint away from the wash. Now it is safe to lay the paper flat again. Allow to dry or dry with a hair dryer.

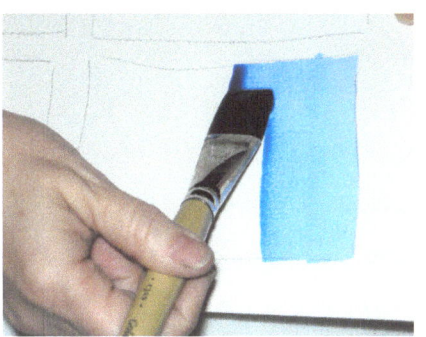

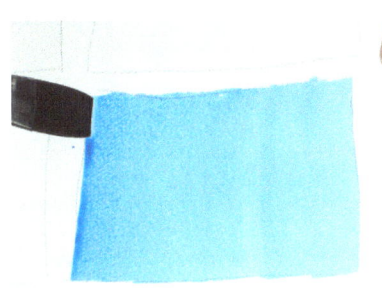

The goal of a flat wash is to create a flat, smooth area of even color.

View a video of this technique at:
http://www.youtube.com/watercolorworks

Graded Wash - A wash that starts with a darker value and progresses to a lighter value.

The same principle that is used for a flat wash is also used in creating a graded wash. The difference is that as each stroke is applied, a small amount of water is added to the brush to make the pigment more diluted. This creates a nice value change, which can be used in almost every painting. It is especially great for skies.

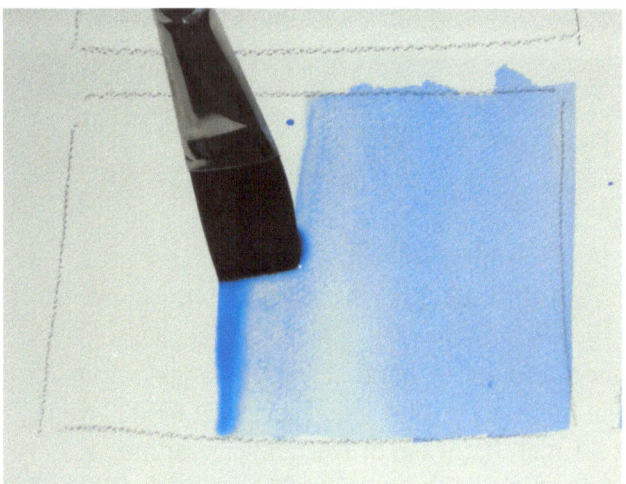 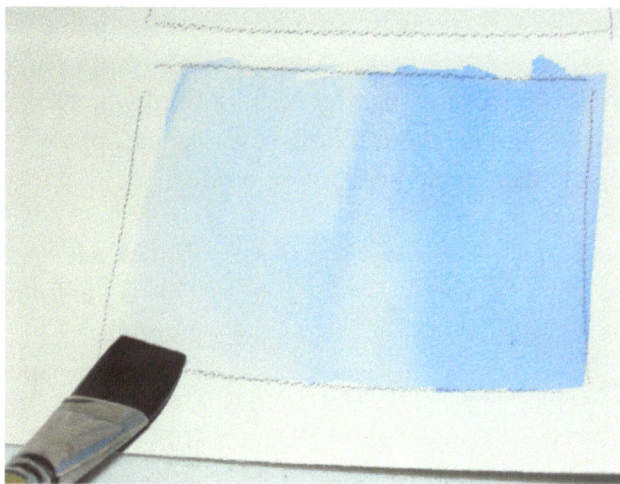

Blended Wash - A wash that contains two or more colors that meet at wet edges to blend together and appear soft.

Again use the same technique to lay down color as you would a flat wash. This time, change pigment part way through. Notice that as the second color touches the bead of the first color, they create a soft edge. If both colors are very wet and the paper is tipped back and forth, they will physically mix to create a soft blend of new color.

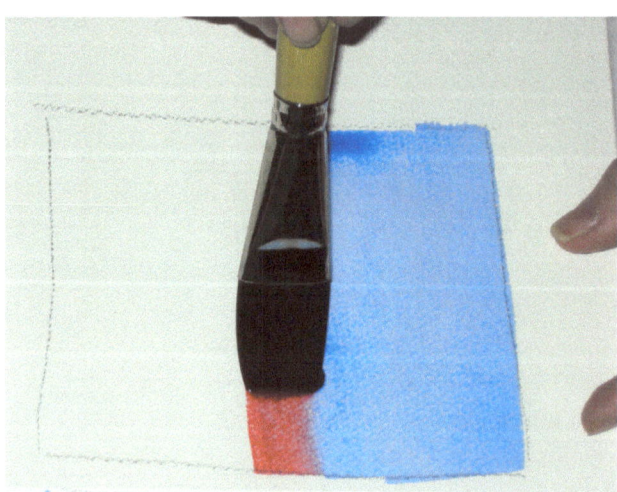 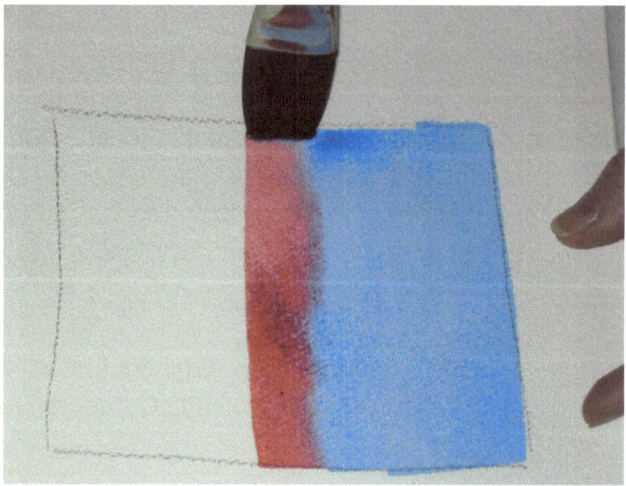

View a video of this technique at:
http://www.youtube.com/watercolorworks

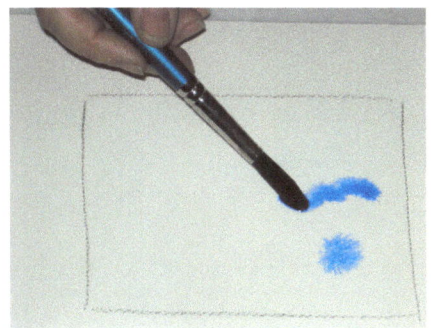 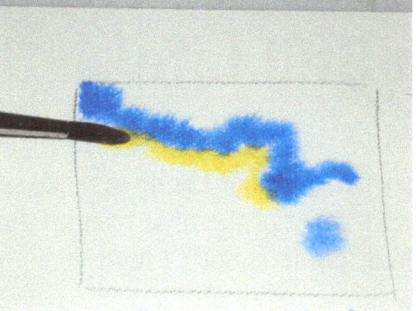 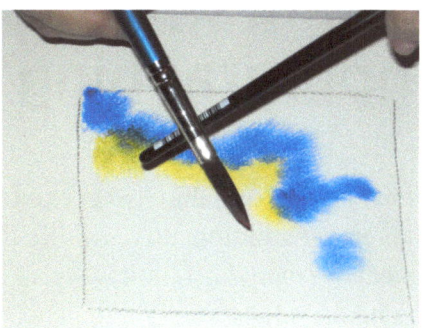

Wet-in-Wet Wash - A varied wash of several colors applied on a wet surface.

Wet-in-wet washes are fun, yet difficult to control. Wet one of your rectangles with plain water or a light color. Completely cover the rectangle. Allow the water to absorb into the paper so there are no standing puddles, but so that there is a glossy appearance.

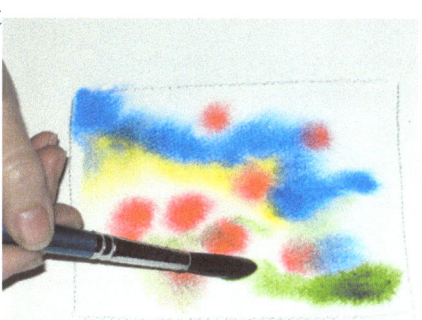

Next, drip or paint strong pigments into the wet areas. Use several colors and experiment. You can also tap a loaded brush onto the handle of another brush to splash pigment into the wetted area. Tipping the paper will blend the colors more, leaving the paper flat will help to contol the blending.

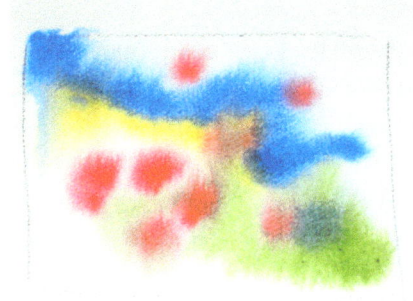

Calligraphic Linework - Linework of pigment developed using all edges of a brush at various angles.

Practice using all of your brushes and see how many marks you can make with each. Hold the brush straight up and down, hold it at a drastic angle, and push and lift it as you pull pigment across the paper. Try to write your name in cursive with each brush you have. Explore what your brushes can do for you!

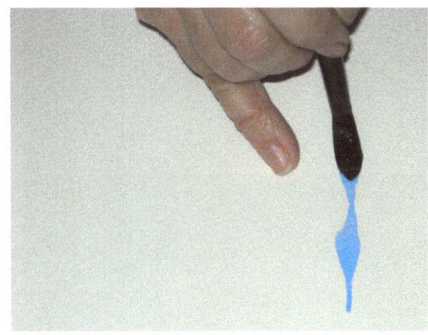 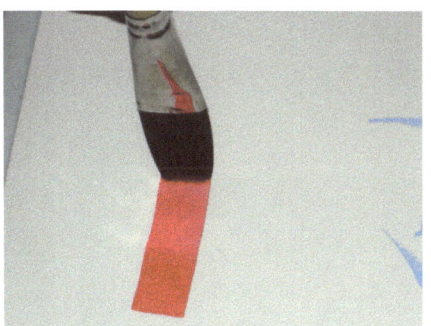 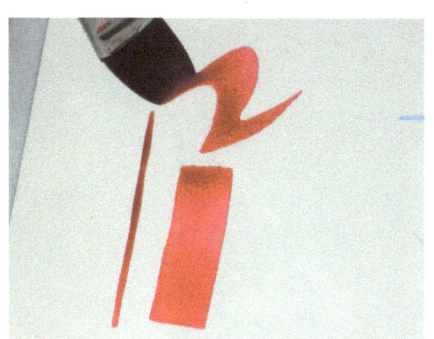

Dry Brush/Scumble - Linework of pigment developed using relatively dry paint and a variety of brush strokes.

View a video of this technique at:
http://www.youtube.com/watercolorworks

Setting Up and Photographing a Still Life

I enjoy collecting things that excite my eye and that I believe make interesting additions to a still life design. Most of the time I set up the objects in many different ways and do a "photo shoot". I rearrange the items, adjust the lighting, and mix things up — all the while using my digital camera to record the process. Some rules of thumb: use

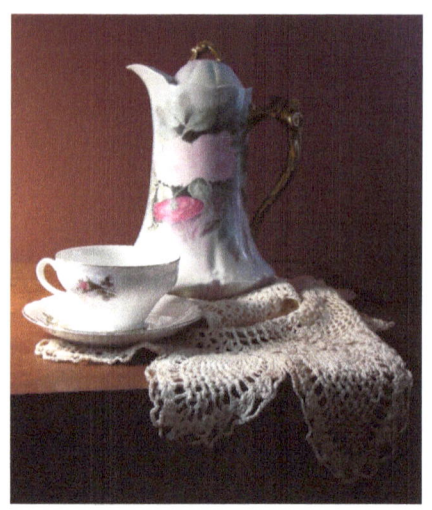

odd numbers of objects, control the light sources so you can have strong lights and shadows, use objects that you enjoy looking at and are familiar with, and keep it simple.

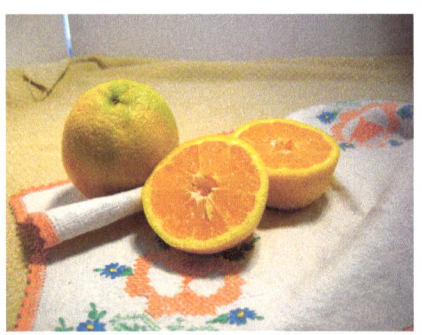

I like to light most of my still life set ups from the upper left. I use cardboard or other objects to block unwanted ambient light sources. I have a small spotlight with a metal reflective top that clamps onto just about anything. It swivels easily so I can control the focal point of the light. I can easily move the light on a set up for a dramatic affect. I also enjoy using fabric, doilies, napkins, and quilts as props along with my objects. They add warmth and interest. It is a good idea to spend a day or two photographing objects to get the right set up, view, and lighting. I work from photos so that I have no time or lighting constraints once I get started in the process of painting.

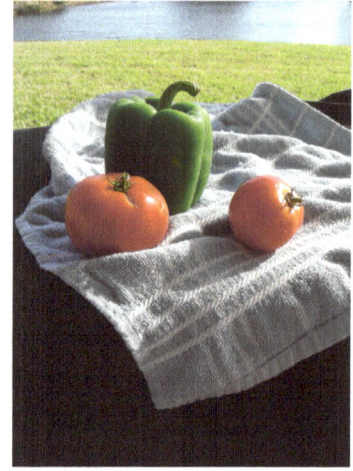

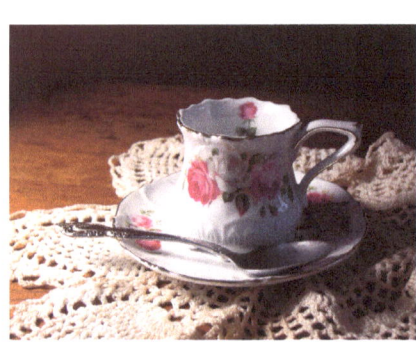

Always use your own photos!!! Collecting and organizing photos is fun and provides rich resources of inspiration for your paintings. I enjoy looking at professional photographs as inspiration for set ups, but I always use my own objects and photos. Once you find photos that suit your desires for a painting it is time to move on to the next step. I have provided reference photos and a final drawing for the project in this book.

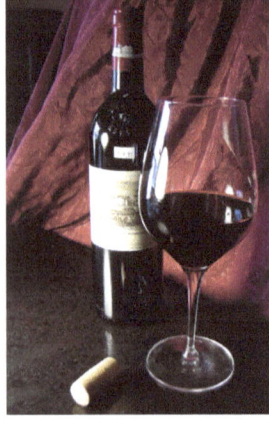

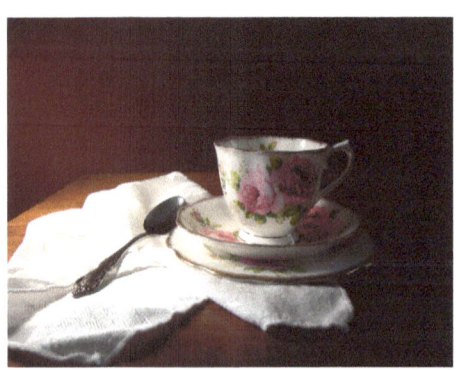

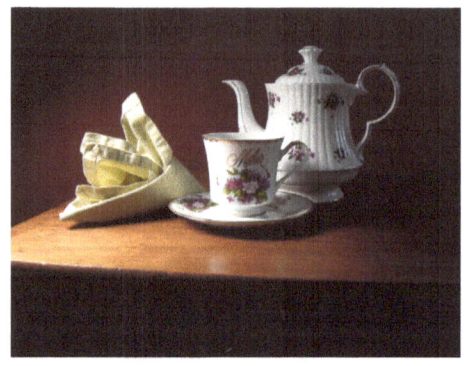

Planning Your Composition

Even though you did a lot of work on your composition at the set up stage, there is still a little more work to do. The more thoroughly you work out the details beforehand the more fun your painting process will become. Whatever problems you neglect to work out at this stage will haunt you throughout the painting.

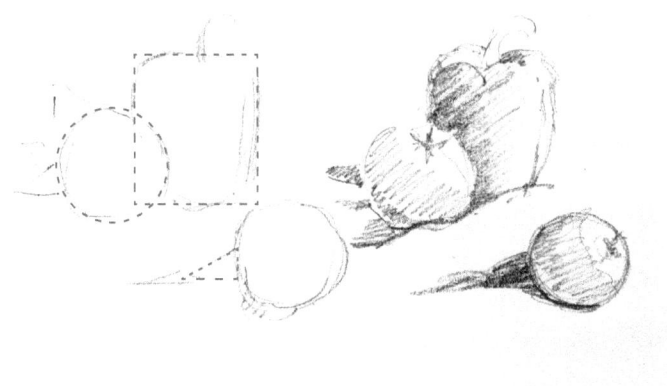

All objects can be reduced to the most basic shapes: circle, square, and triangle. From those basic shapes we can add shading and distortion to make cones, rectangles, cylinders, ovals, etc. These simple shapes are found everywhere.

Try to sketch the most basic shapes (triangles, cones, squares, ovals, etc.) from your composition in your sketchbook. Place the objects in a pleasing way on your paper. Don't worry about any details until the basic shapes are in the correct place.

Now you will develop some thumbnail sketches from your basic shapes. Thumbnail sketches should be small and should be used for problem solving before you ever touch your watercolor paper. They are quick, sketchy little drawings of the basic shapes you are looking at. They help you to quickly move objects around your picture plane, work on value contrast and develop a basic composition for your painting.

Remember to minimize the shapes to help you work quickly. This is not a final drawing, just a method to work out the most important aspects of your painting: composition and value. If your composition and values are right, your painting will be a success.

Things to think about while developing thumbnail sketches:
• Do I want to make this painting in a horizontal or vertical format?
• Do I want all of the objects to appear in whole or do I want to cut some off at the edges?
• How can I add more interest?
• Is this painting flat or are there interesting changes in plane, line and position?
• Where is my horizon line?
• What are the basic shapes of the objects I want to add to my painting?
• How do the sizes of the shapes relate to one another?
• Are the distant objects smaller than the closer objects?
• How dark or light are the objects compared to each other?
• Where do I want the focal point or point of interest in my painting to be?
• How can I draw the viewers interest to the focal point? Use details, color, value contrast?
• Is this a subject that will keep me interested the entire time I work on it?
• What details can I leave out of this piece?
• What details are essential to the piece?
• Is this painting telling a story, expressing an idea, telling something about the artist, or simply painted for the pleasure of painting?
• Is there a dominant color in the painting?
• Are the colors leaning toward cool or warm?
• Is there a strong sense of light and dark to define the volume of the shapes?

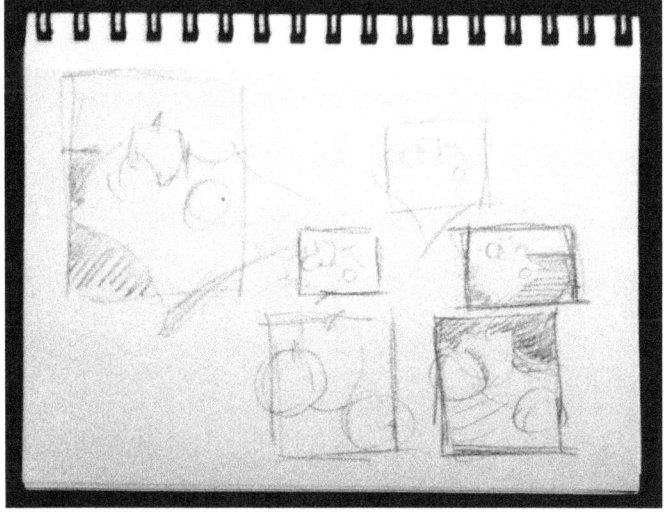

Thumbnail Sketch Process

1. Look for the basic shapes in your composition.
- Is it a triangle shape, a round shape, a rectangular shape?
- Is it bigger on top than the bottom?
- Is it pear-shaped?
- Is it soft-edged, crisp, or angular?
- Are some objects overlapping?
- Are there spaces between objects?
- What shapes are the "empty" areas.
- Where does it fall in the picture plane? (Hint: draw a grid to help locate specific elements and get their relationship to one another and to the paper edges correct.)

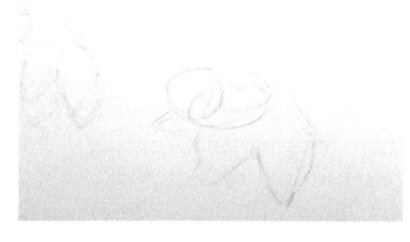

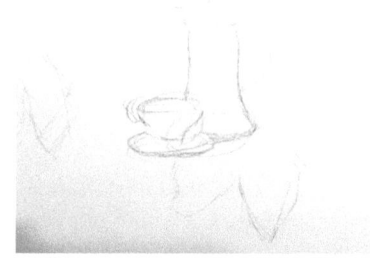

2. After capturing the basic outer shape of the objects, and placement on the picture plane, ask yourself the same questions from step 1 about the individual parts: shadow shapes, cup handles, folds in fabric. Also ask:
- Do the objects reach up or swing out and down?
- Are they close together or is there a bit of space between them?
- Is there a crisp edge to the shadow shape or does it gently grade from dark to light?
- Are the shapes correctly sized compared to each other?

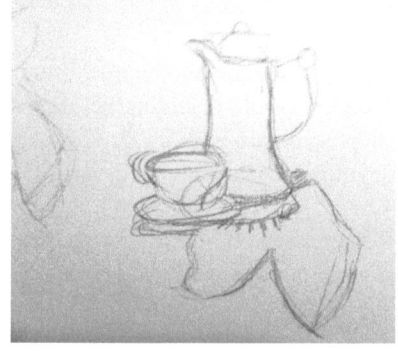

3. Now think in values.
- Use your value scale* and think light = value 1; dark = value 6.
- Mark the numbers 1 - 6 on your thumbnail to relate to the values.
- If you have combined photo references for a better composition, decide the values for the added elements.
- Pay attention to areas in shadow and in light.
- Shade in the values according to your numbers with a pencil.

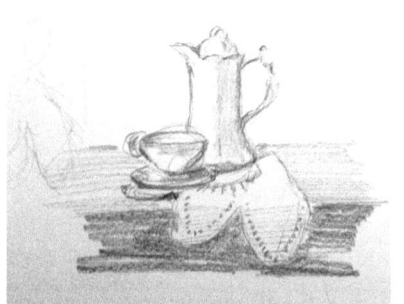

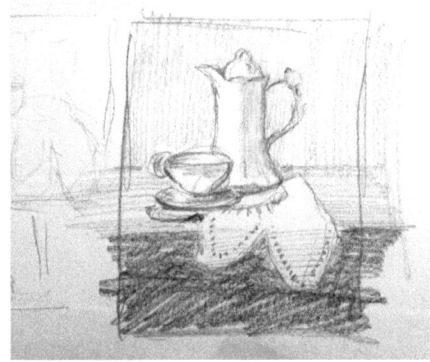

Thumbnail sketches are not final drawings. They are simply a method to work out solutions to common composition and value problems. Focus not on drawing but on the most basic elements of the picture.

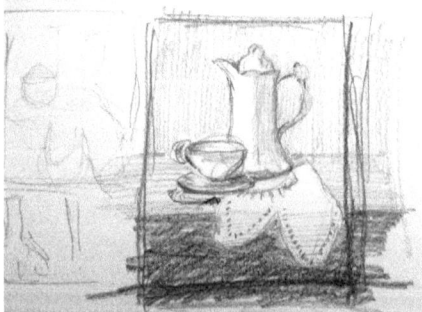

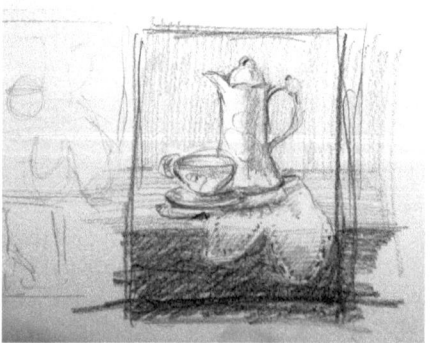

* A Value Scale is available in the photo references section in this book.

Preparing a Drawing

There are lots of ways to develop drawings for your paintings. Once you have developed a thumbnail sketch that you think fits your goals for the painting you can then make a larger drawing to match the size of your desired finished painting. Use this drawing to transfer to your watercolor paper.

Many of my students don't enjoy the drawing process as much as painting or simply don't have strong drawing skills, so I help them to find simpler, easier ways to develop their drawings. Many fine, professional watercolor artists use slides or computers to help them in this process. Others use a grid system, which works very well. Others simply rely on the basics in their thumbnail sketches to get the simple ideas down, then paint in a looser fashion, not worrying about the details at all.

If you have strong drawing skills, I believe that producing the drawing by hand from your references and thumbnails is the best approach. If you are anxious to paint, or don't have strong drawing skills, you can make a small drawing by tracing your photos over a light box, or hold them up to a brightly lit window. Then, when you have the basic shapes and some of the details you want to capture in your drawing

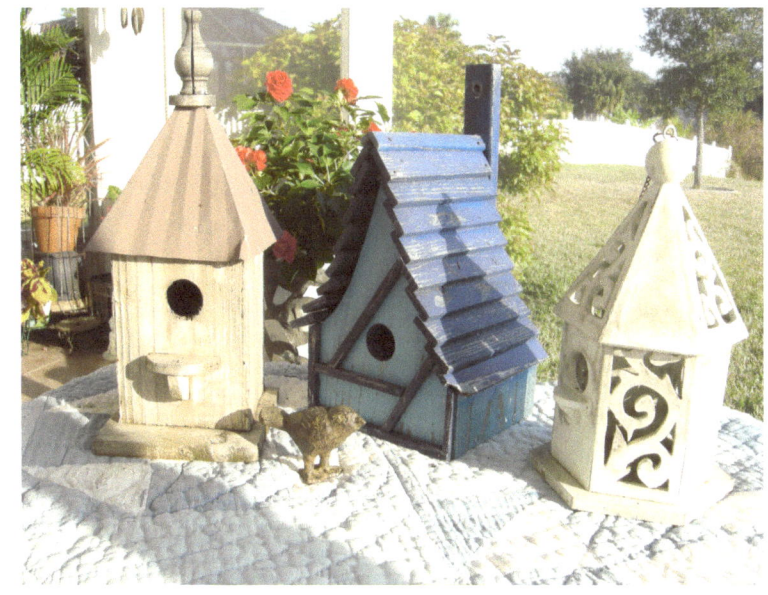

you can use a photocopier to enlarge the components and place them on the proper size drawing paper for your desired painting.

No matter how you prepare your drawing, the point that you develop it through sketching and study is crucial to a successful painting. This is the stage where you work out the road map for your painting. Take the time to sketch and get intimately familiar with the shapes and values of all the objects you want in your painting. You may even want to develop small watercolor sketches of the piece to work out color problems that may arise.

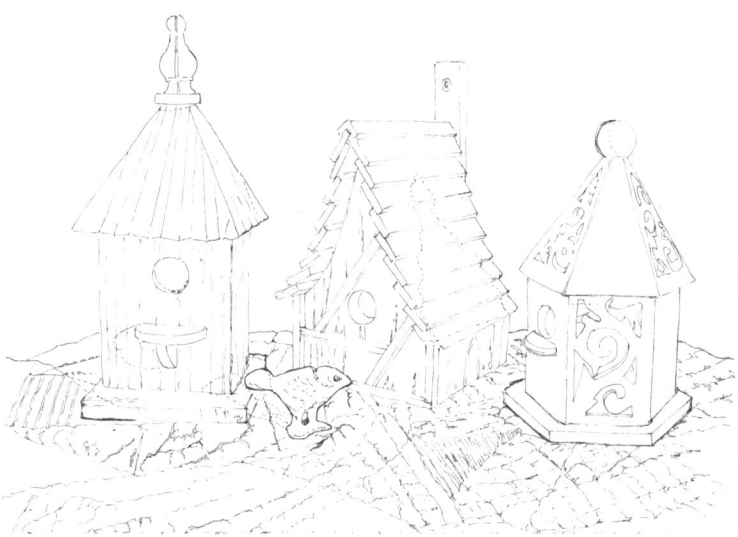

Now that you have a developed drawing, let's transfer it to your prepared watercolor paper.

Remember, the drawing should be the exact size of the desired finished painting, or the same size as your watercolor sheet.

How to Prepare Watercolor Paper

What you will need:

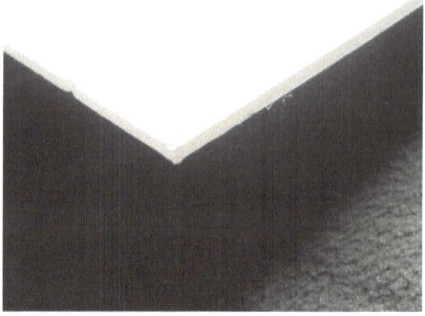

- Foam core board at least two to three inches bigger than your watercolor paper on all sides.
- Clear Packing Tape
- Two Inch Wide Masking Tape
- Scissors
- Watercolor Paper

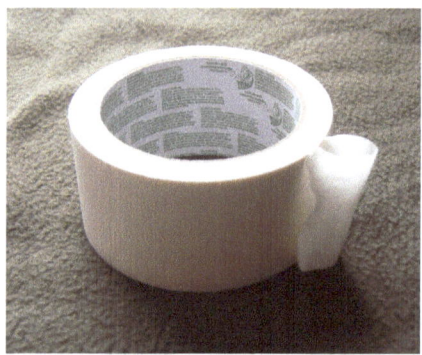

Some artists stretch wet paper onto heavy boards to keep the sheets flat while painting. I prefer this simple method of mounting dry paper onto foam core board to maintain the integrity of my paper while painting.

The process that I use protects the areas of the foam core board where you will eventually tape your watercolor paper. The clear packing tape prevents the masking tape from tearing the foam core and it slightly waterproofs the edges to protect it when applying juicy washes onto your painting. This board, if properly prepared, will be useful for many paintings in the future. It is a lightweight alternative to the traditional method of stretching watercolor paper.

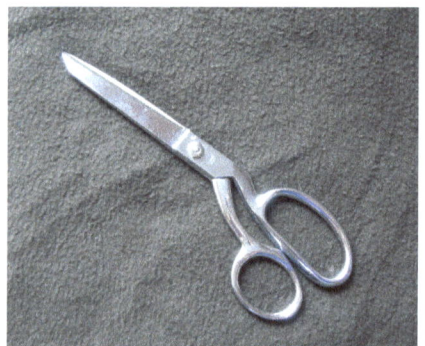

1. Cut foam core so that it measures about two to three inches larger than your watercolor paper on all sides.

2. Tape the outer edges of the foam core with clear packing tape. Cover the edges with at least two rows of tape on all sides, front and back. This board may be used over and over again as a support for your watercolor paper.

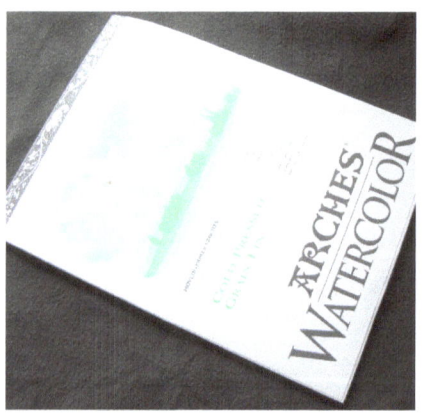

3. Tape watercolor paper to prepared foam core board with masking tape. Be sure that at least 1/2 inch of your watercolor paper is covered with the tape to secure it to the board. Remember, your paper will get wet while painting. This will cause it to buckle, warp, and stretch. The secure application of tape will hold it firmly to the foam core during the painting process.

4. Now you are ready to transfer a drawing to your paper.

Your framer will appreciate the fact that your artwork was stretched to stay more flat. Framing a warped and bowed watercolor is very difficult.

Transfer the Drawing to Watercolor Paper

What you will need:
- Watercolor paper
- Completed drawing and thumbnail sketches
- Photo references
- Chunky graphite stick
- Pencil for tracing
- Prepared foam core stabilizer board
- Two inch wide masking tape

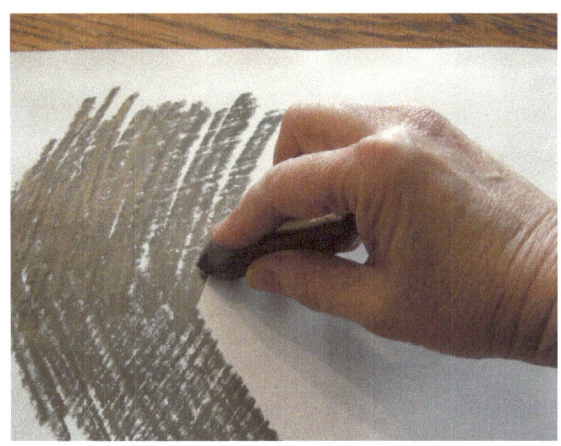

1. Scrub the chunky graphite stick on the back of your completed drawing. Use a little elbow grease to get good coverage over the entire image area.

2. Use a tissue to gently smooth over the graphite to release loose crumbs and to fill in the spaces where the graphite didn't completely cover the paper. Use a light touch.

3. Wash your hands! This will keep your watercolor paper clean.

4. Use a strip of masking tape and secure the drawing on one edge to your watercolor paper, like a hinge. This will allow you to lift the drawing occasionally to check your progress, without losing your alignment.

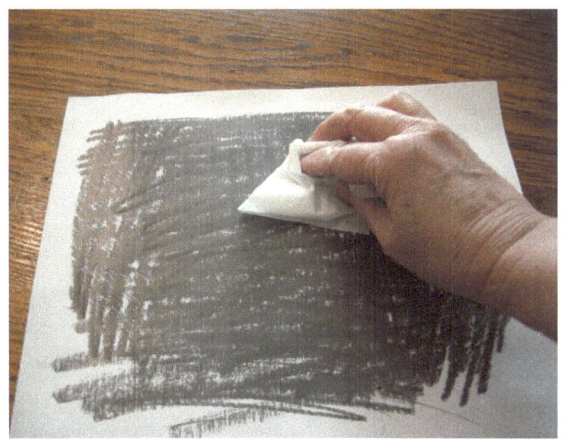

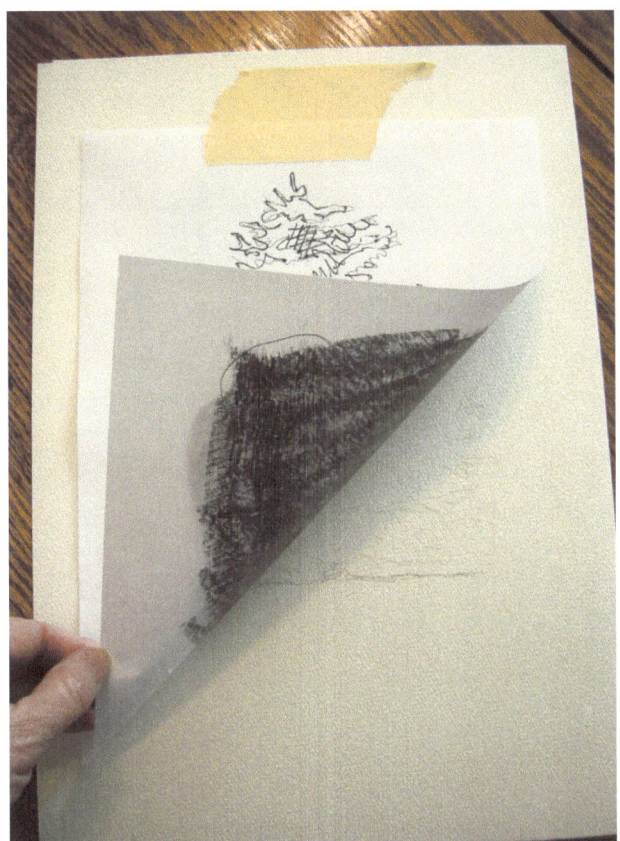

5. Trace your image using a pencil or an ink pen. Be gentle so that you do not dent the watercolor paper. You only need to press enough to deposit the graphite image lightly onto the paper.

6. Carefully lift off the drawing paper and fold it in half so that the graphite is on the inside of the fold.

7. Now you can use a pencil to correct any markings you may want to fix. Using a white vinyl eraser you may also gently erase places where you don't want the graphite.

8. Place your watercolor paper on the prepared foam core board. Secure it with the masking tape. Be sure to cover at least 1/2 inch of the paper edges with the tape to keep it from buckling when wet.

9. Now you are ready to paint!!!

An alternative method is to use graphite transfer paper purchased from an art supply store.

Let's Paint!

I worked on the drawing and then I traced it onto my watercolor paper. I used Arches 300 pound cold press paper.

I used two inch masking tape and adhered all edges of the paper to my prepared foam core base. Be sure that at least 1/2 inch of the watercolor paper is covered with tape all around. If you tape less than a 1/2 inch, chances are the tape will not hold when you apply the wet washes of color and the paper will be buckled even after drying.

Use the transfer process described in previous pages or use graphite transfer paper. Do not use carbon paper!

The drawing and photo references for this project may be found at the back of this book.

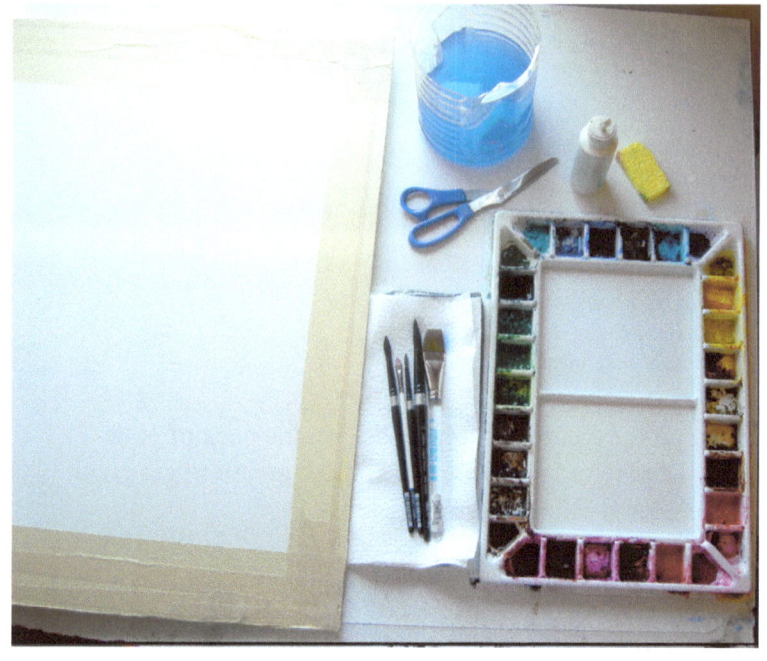

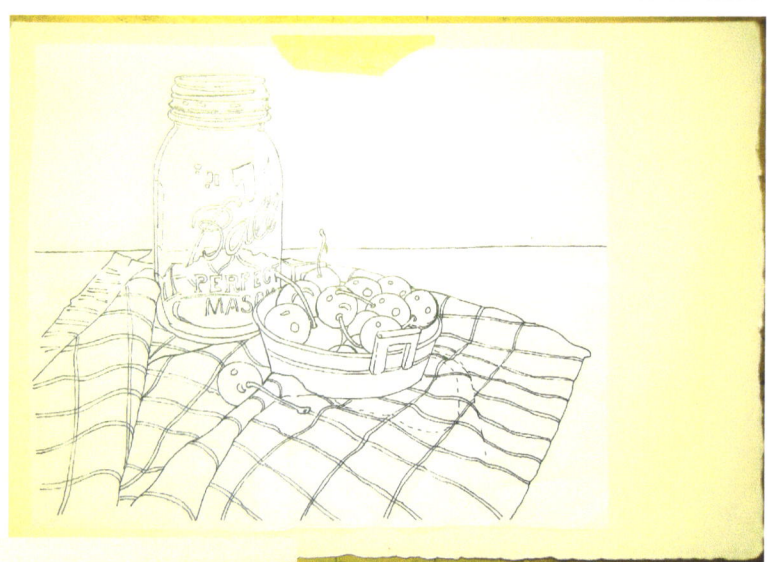

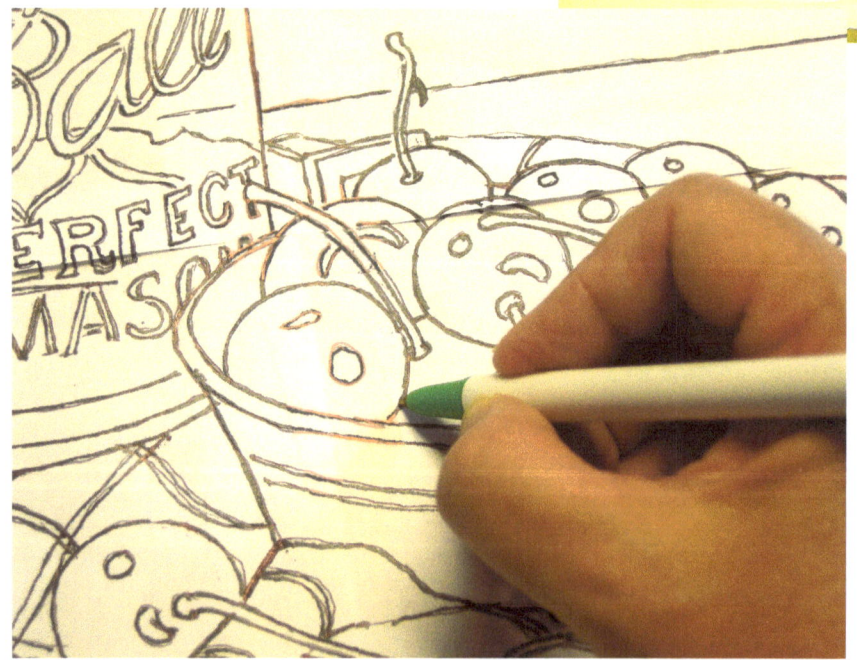

I often use a red ink pen to trace my drawing so that I can easily keep track of which lines I have already traced. Be sure to use a light hand so that you do not dent the watercolor paper which will make areas where pigment will pool and be challenging to control.

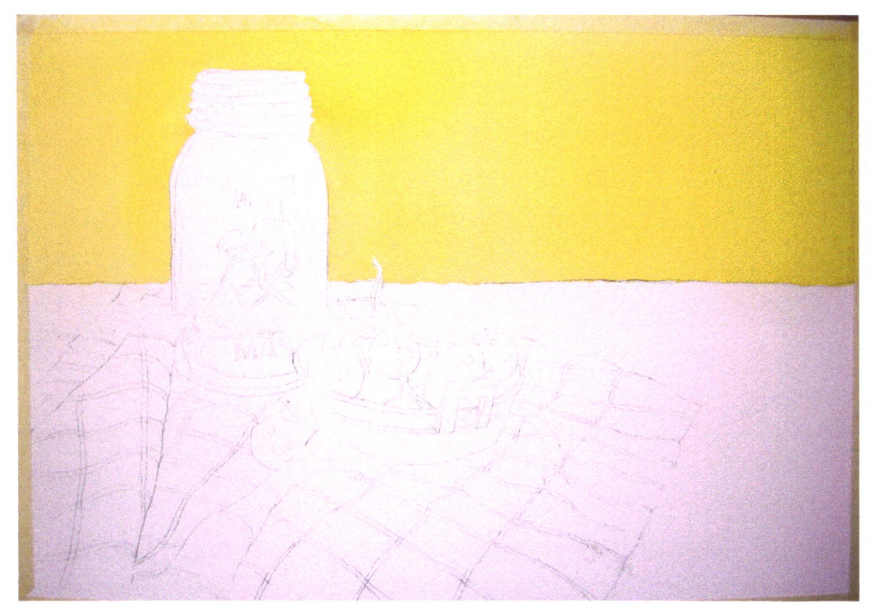

I like to begin with my largest washes, and I often start with the first glaze of a background wash. I used a large, wet puddle of Aureolin Yellow and New Gamboge to wash onto the background. Keep the board tipped. Use a one or two inch flat wash brush and stroke each area only once. Allow gravity and water to make the pigment flow. If you use a very light touch on the paper, only using the brush to direct the puddle, your paper will not be disturbed and your washes will be clean and bright.

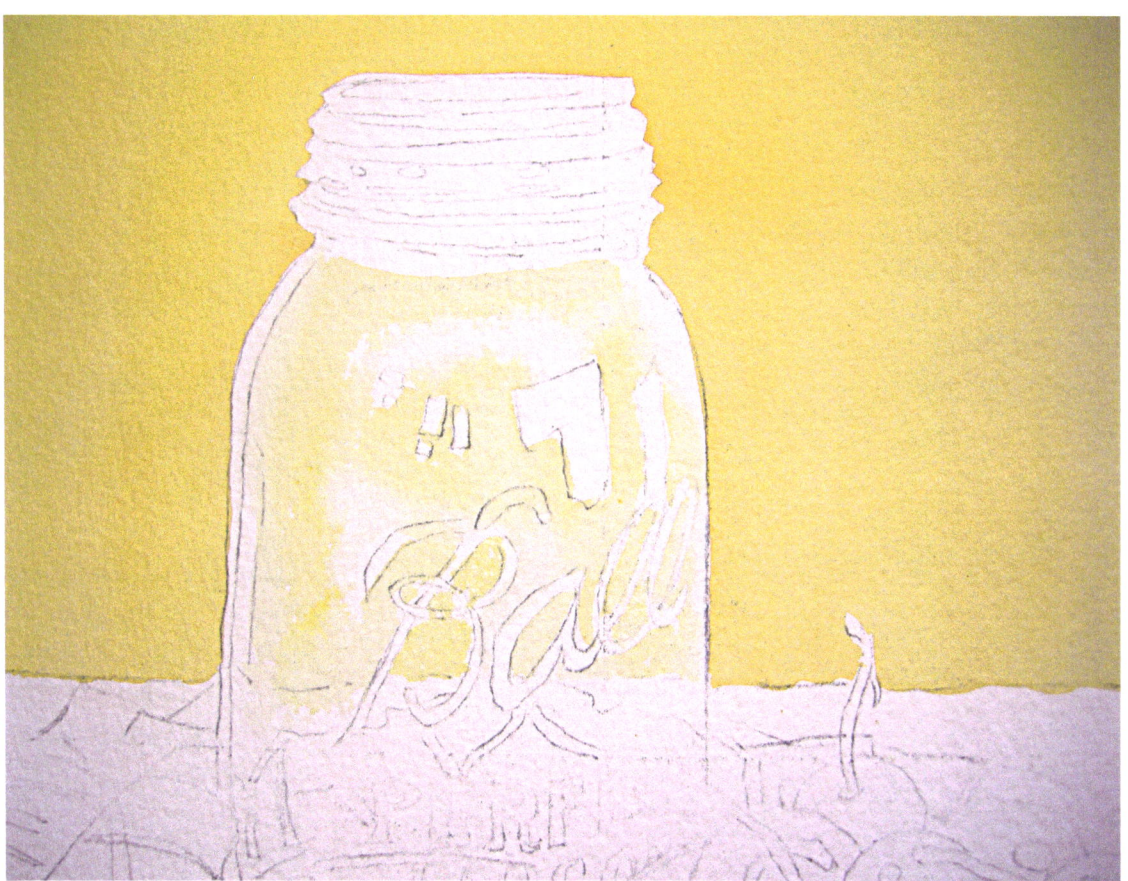

I also added some of this mixture to the areas in the jar where I can see the background showing through. Notice the use of soft edges and crisp edges.

View a video of this technique at:
http://www.youtube.com/watercolorworks

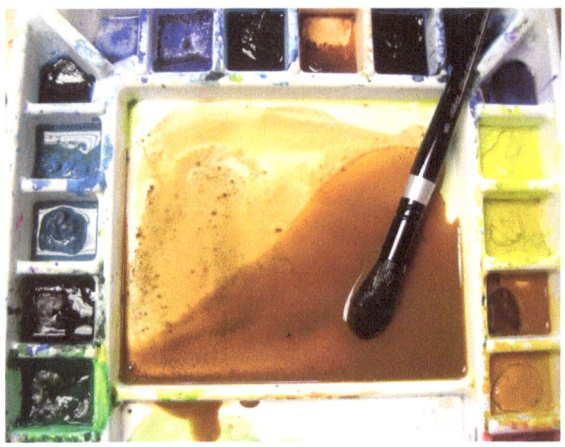

Now it is time to add some Burnt Sienna to the puddle of yellows that was used earlier. Again I wanted to work in the largest basic washes first, so I painted a foundational layer of paint for the table. I mixed a large puddle and used lots of water. The wetter the wash the nicer it will flow when applied to the paper.

Because I work very wet, there is usually a bead of paint at the end of the wash. I use a piece of paper toweling to gently touch along the taped edge of the painting. You can also just touch the

paper toweling to the puddle, without even touching the paper. This will siphon off the extra liquid so that it will not run back into the wash and create a bloom.

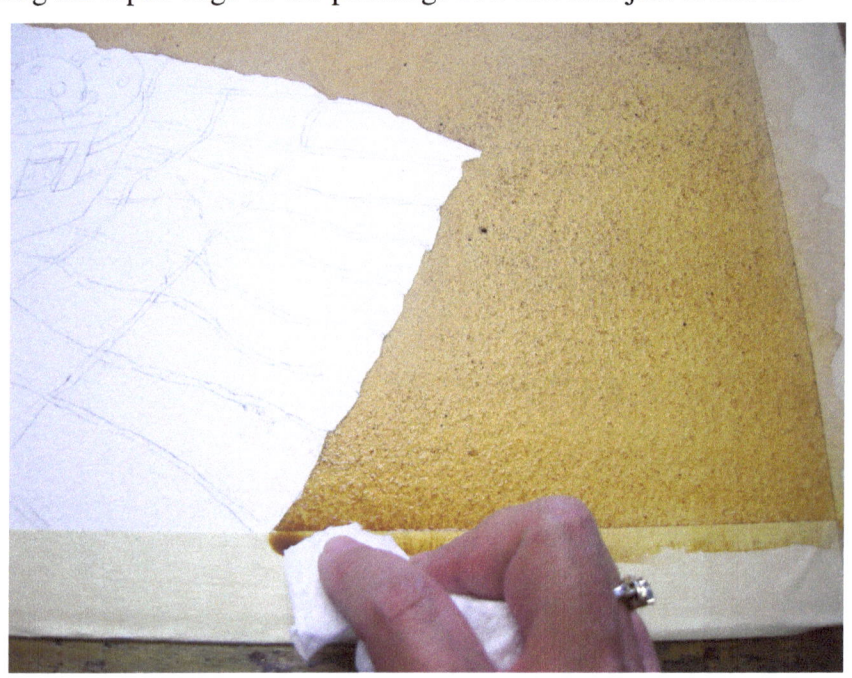

Paint the largest areas first, then go back and paint the table where it shows through the jar. Because the glass will distort the line, it should not line up perfectly with the normal view of the jar.

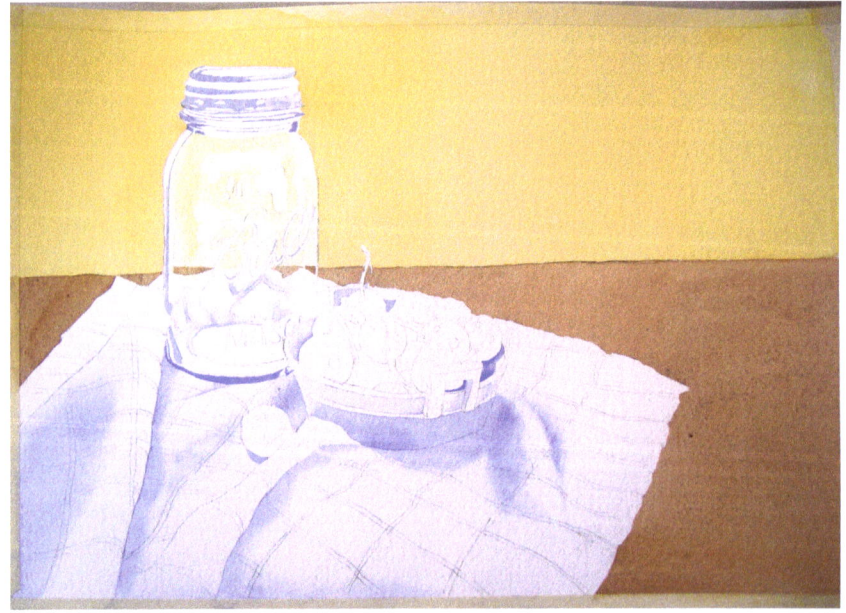

Using French Ultramarine Blue I painted in the shadowed areas of my still life. I like to do this for several reasons. This helps to establish the foundation, or bones, of the painting. It also helps me to identify which direction the light is coming from and it creates an under-layer of cool color where I want the shadows to appear. You will see why this is so important very soon.

To create the soft edges of color on the towel and in some of the other shadow areas, I used what I call my Softened Edge Stroke. I apply a nice, rich, wet stroke of color in a small area, then clean the brush with clear water and tamp it on the paper toweling. I use the clean damp brush to pull a tiny bit of moisture into the stroke of color. The moistened edge creates a soft edge. It is very important to push the liquid into the pigment and not to pull the pigment out into the clean, wet area. Pushing the water into the colored stroke will help to create a soft edge that does not have a funky line of dried pigment, because the water softens the edge to the white of the paper. If you have any pigment in that edge it will look dirty and ruin the transition of dark to light.

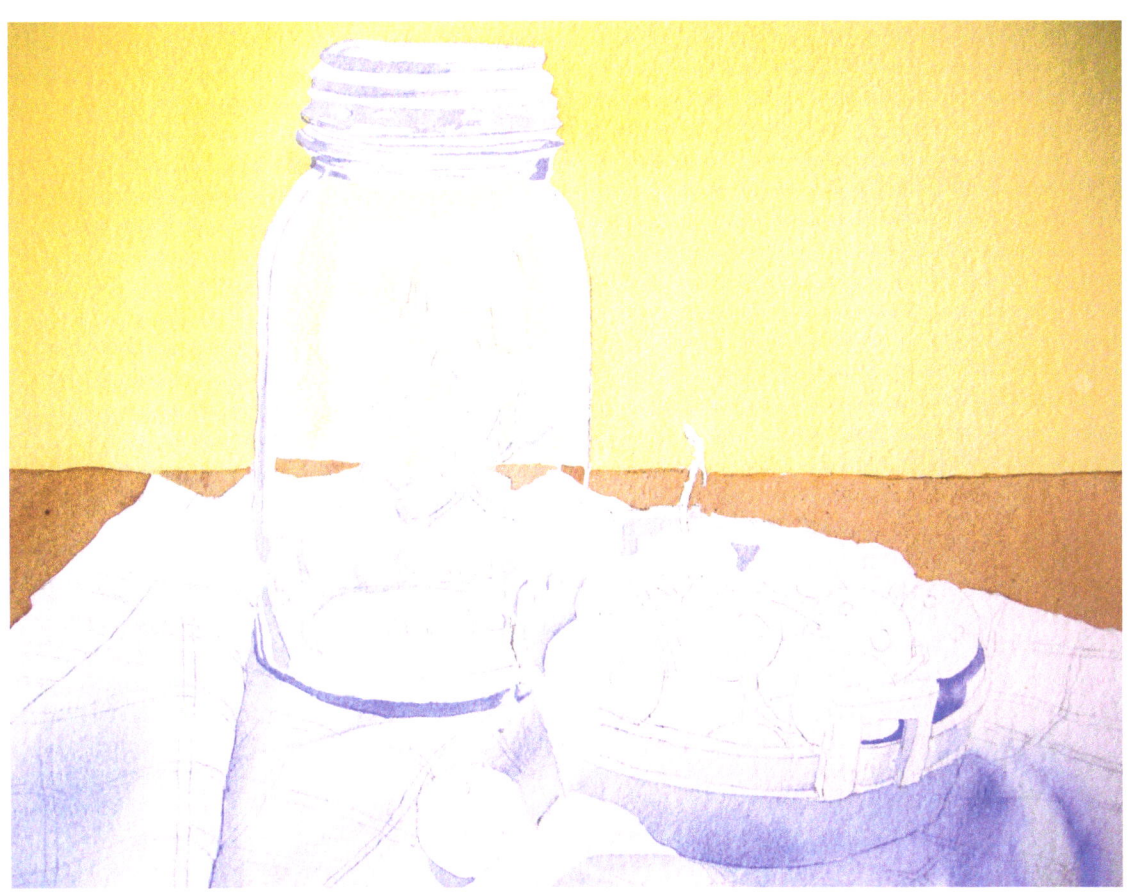

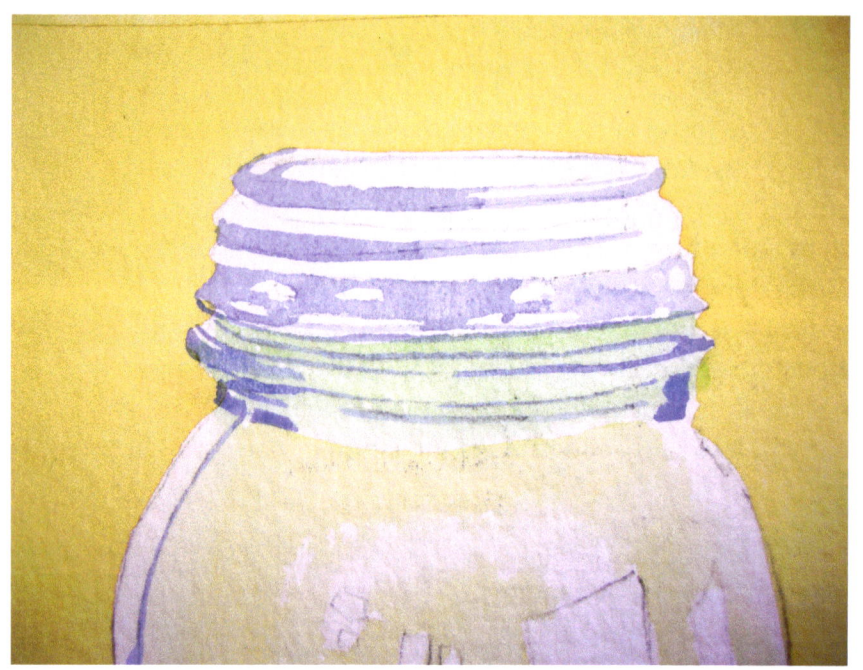

I used Sap Green to add a wet wash of color to several areas on the jar. I again used the Softened Edge Stroke to create soft glazes. I used different strengths of color (by using different mixtures of pigment and water) to develop some darker values and some lighter values. It's important to use your photo reference and thumbnail studies as keys. They will guide you as to where you need color, what shapes those colors should be applied, and how dark or light the color should appear.

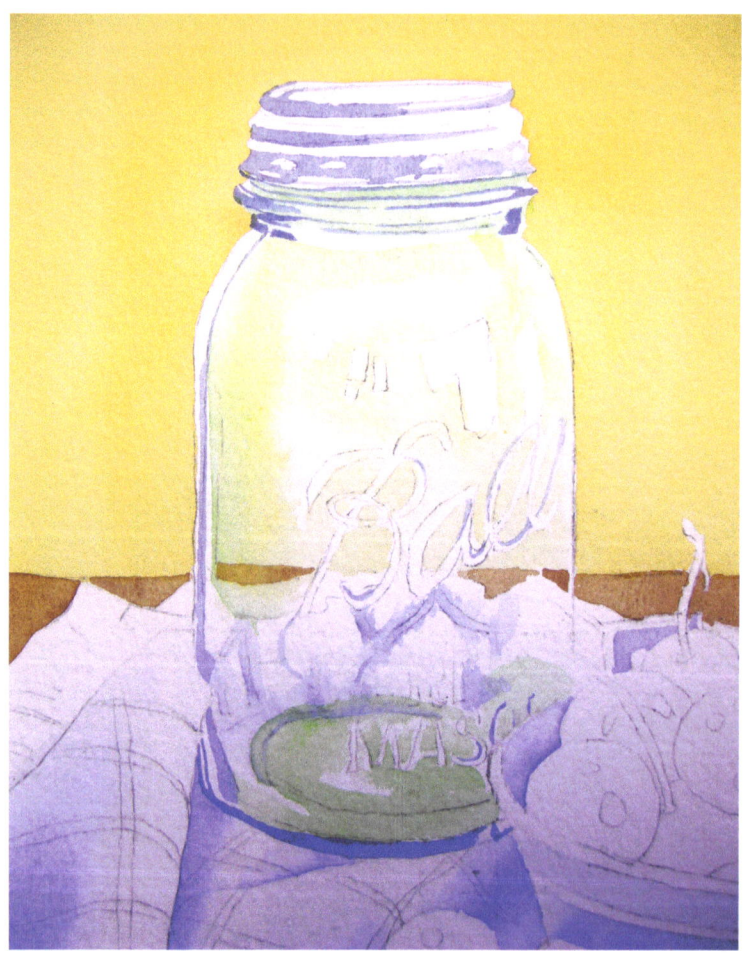

Because the previous glazes of color were bone dry, the soft application of another color on top of the previous layers creates a depth of color that cannot be achieved otherwise. When glazing several layers of color, be sure to use a very light touch and do not brush too much. Extensive brushing will simply lift and mix the colors and create mud. Each layer of color should be applied only after the previous layer is completely dry.

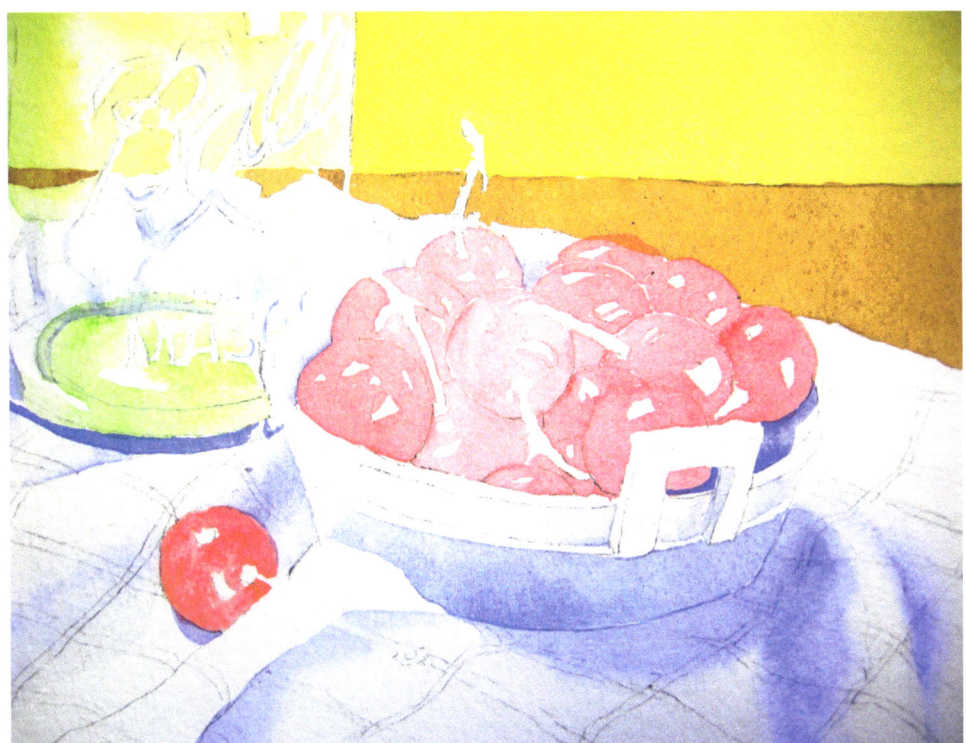

Take a look at the red pigments on your palette. Each red has either a warm or cool cast to it. I used a very wet wash of Winsor Red on the cherries to provide a base color for the subsequent glazes. This is about 90 percent water and 10 percent pigment — very wet. I did not mask the highlights in the cherries for this painting, so I painted around them. If you have a difficult time with painting around those tiny areas, you may want to add a little masking fluid first.

I have left a tiny little white area around all of the cherries at this point to create a separation between them visually. Later on I will fill this in with shadow color, but for now I will leave the white area. It also helps me to see where each cherry begins and ends because as I work with the wet paint it will often lift the graphite and the pencil lines will disappear.

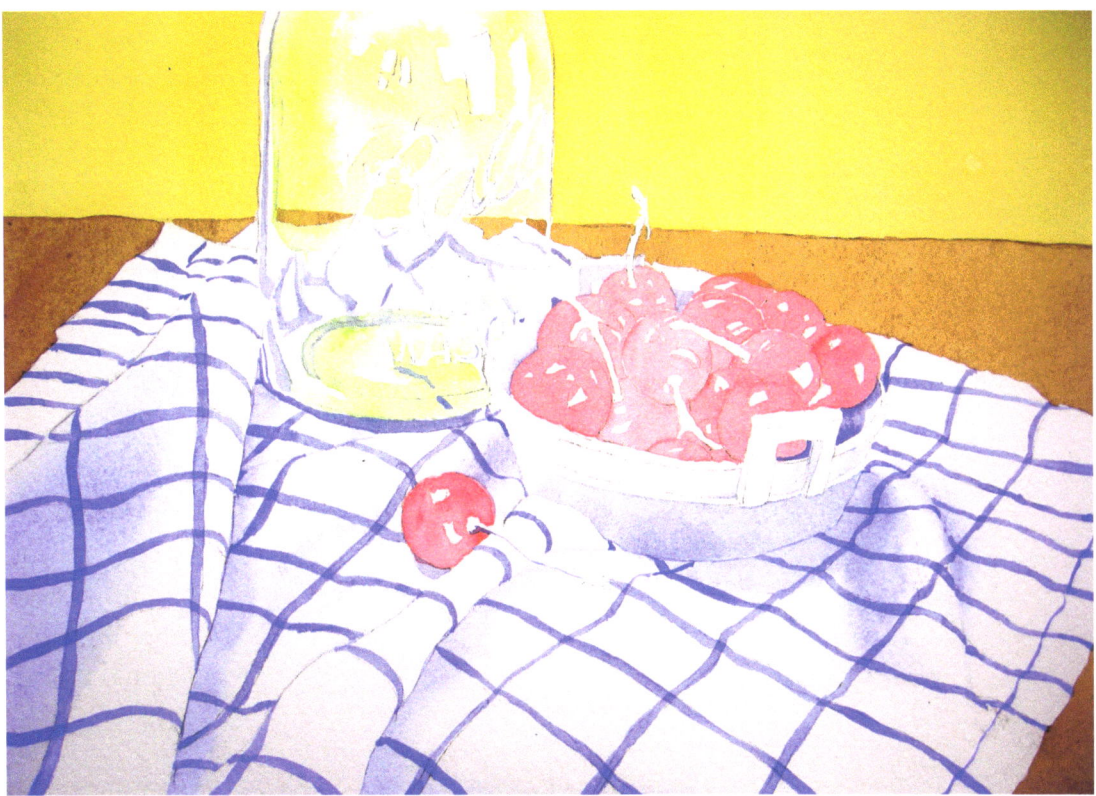

Using French Ultramarine Blue, I added the lines on the towel. I tried to create each line with as few brush strokes as possible. This keeps the painting looking fresh and painterly. It's okay if the lines are not perfect. The towel is not the focal point for this painting. Too much detail, even in detailed work, becomes fussy-looking. Besides, the viewer's eyes will put it all together. If you add every single detail the painting will lose its sparkle and life and will appear boring.

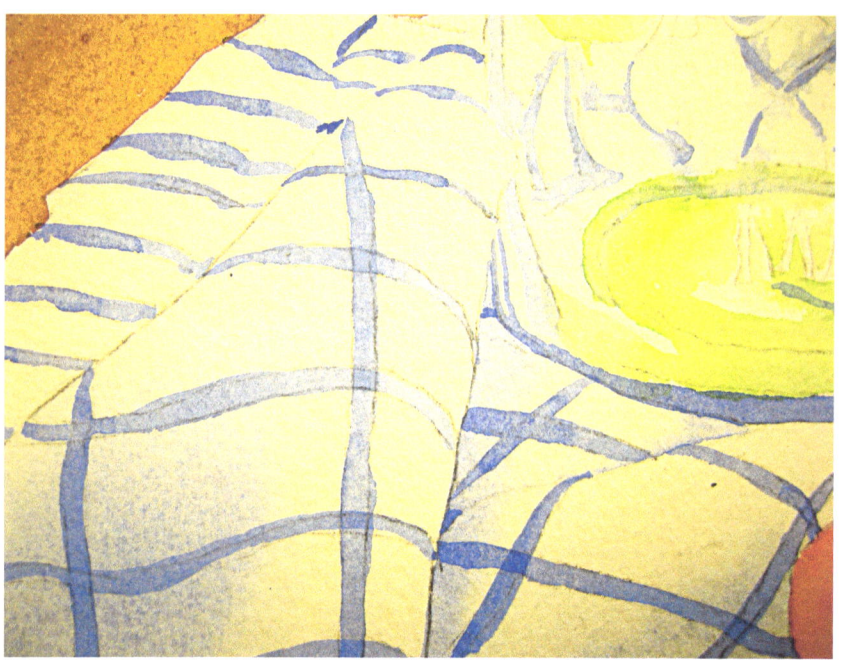

I returned to the French Ultramarine Blue and used a very wet wash of color on the folded edges of the towel. As before, I used my Softened Edge Stroke to create a soft edge where I don't want a crisp line in the color.

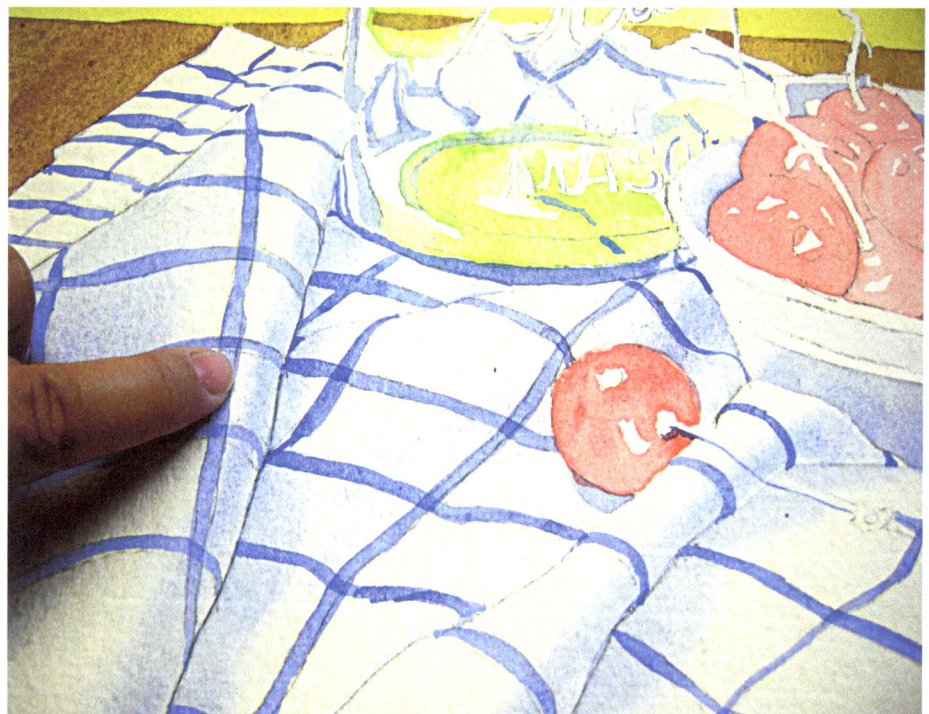

Pay attention to the lightness and darkness (values) of the different shadow areas. The shadows will be darker on one side. There is also some light bouncing around the objects. Squint your eyes to see the different values. In your photo references you will see that one photo is printed in black and white. This also helps to identify the subtle, different values throughout the piece without being distracted by color. Remember to look for the abstract, simple shapes, and then watch for different value changes. This makes the illusion of a three-dimensional object.

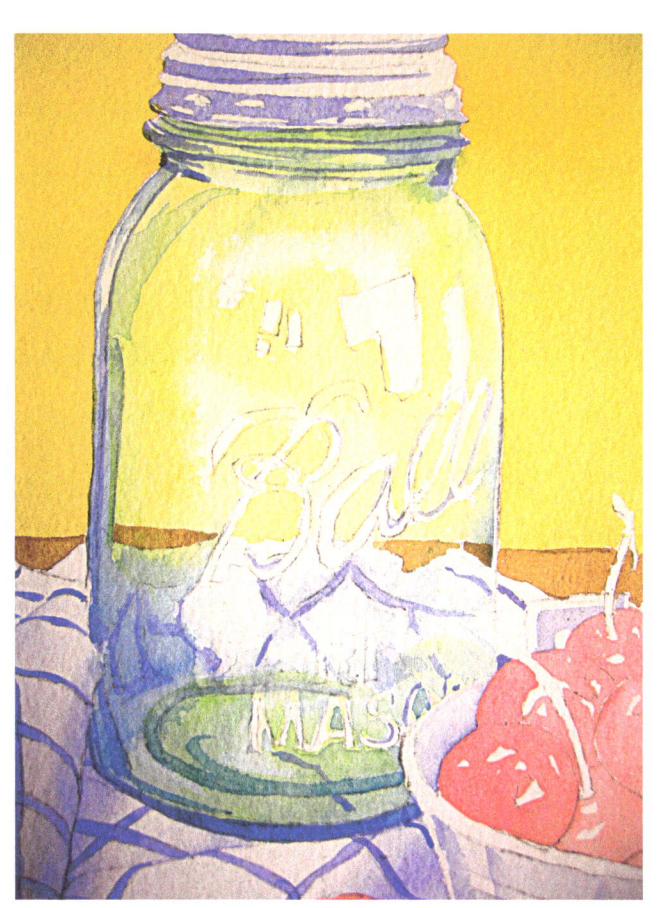

Next I used French Ultramarine Blue to develop the subtle light effects in the glass. I added some very wet pigments to the jar, and to the white bowl. Notice how the towel reflects into the shiny glass. Keep the applications light and wet. Use both crisp and soft edges, letting your reference be your guide.

Be sure to allow each area to dry before you paint into it again. In the canning jar, I painted the shadows on some of the letters. It is very crucial to not allow yourself to get too literal here. Pick out one value, the darkest value, and don't allow yourself to work in any lighter values yet. You also don't have to paint everything you see. This is where the artist in you will learn to filter out what is necessary to the painting and what can be left out!

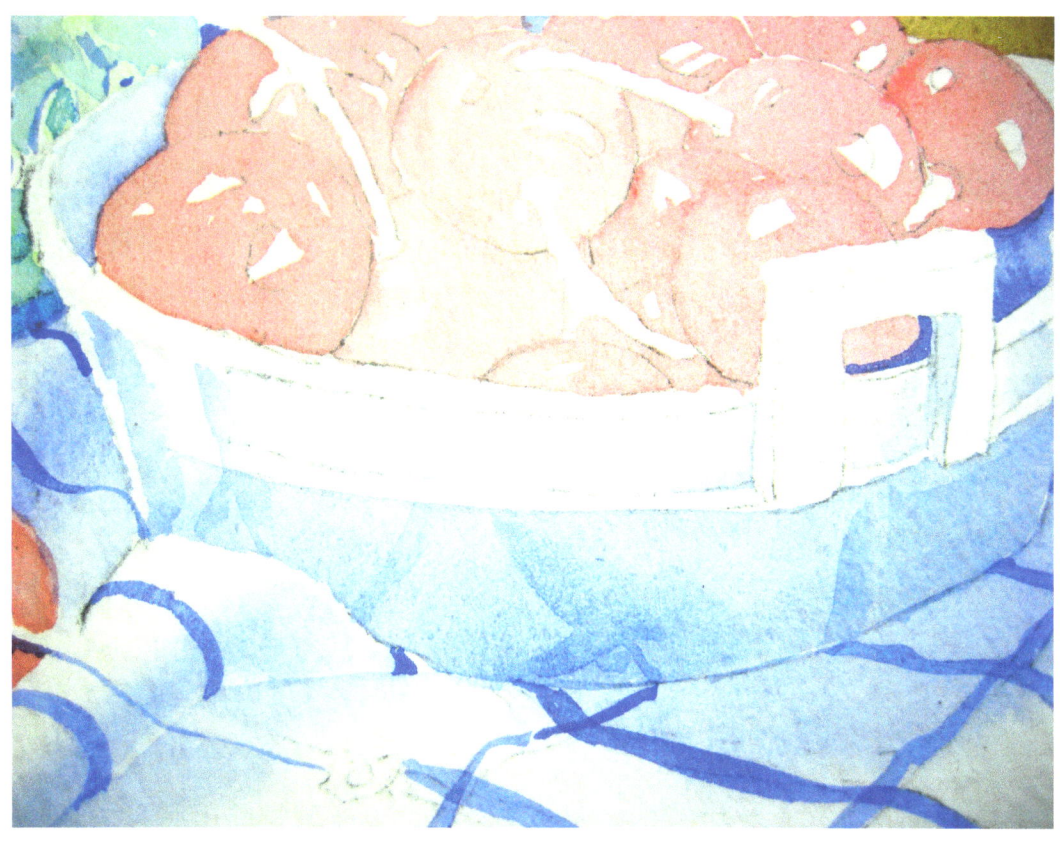

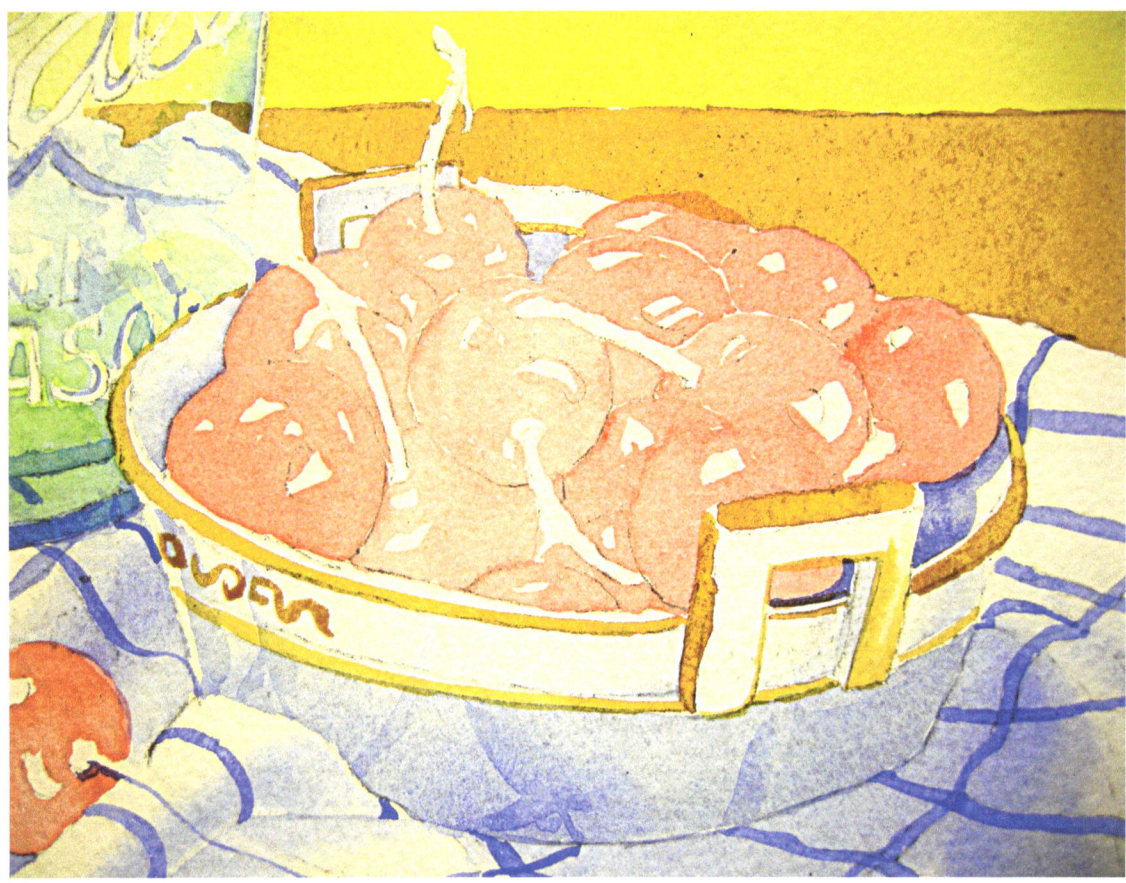

Using a wet mixture of Quinacridone Gold and Burnt Sienna, I have touched in some of the gold edges on the dish. I used varying mixtures of these colors. Where you see a lighter value in your photo reference, paint it lighter with more water. Where you see a darker value in the reference, paint it darker with more pigment. To make it darker in value use a slightly stronger pigment and perhaps use more Burnt Sienna than gold. It is amazing to me how different the piece begins to look with this addition of warm colors!

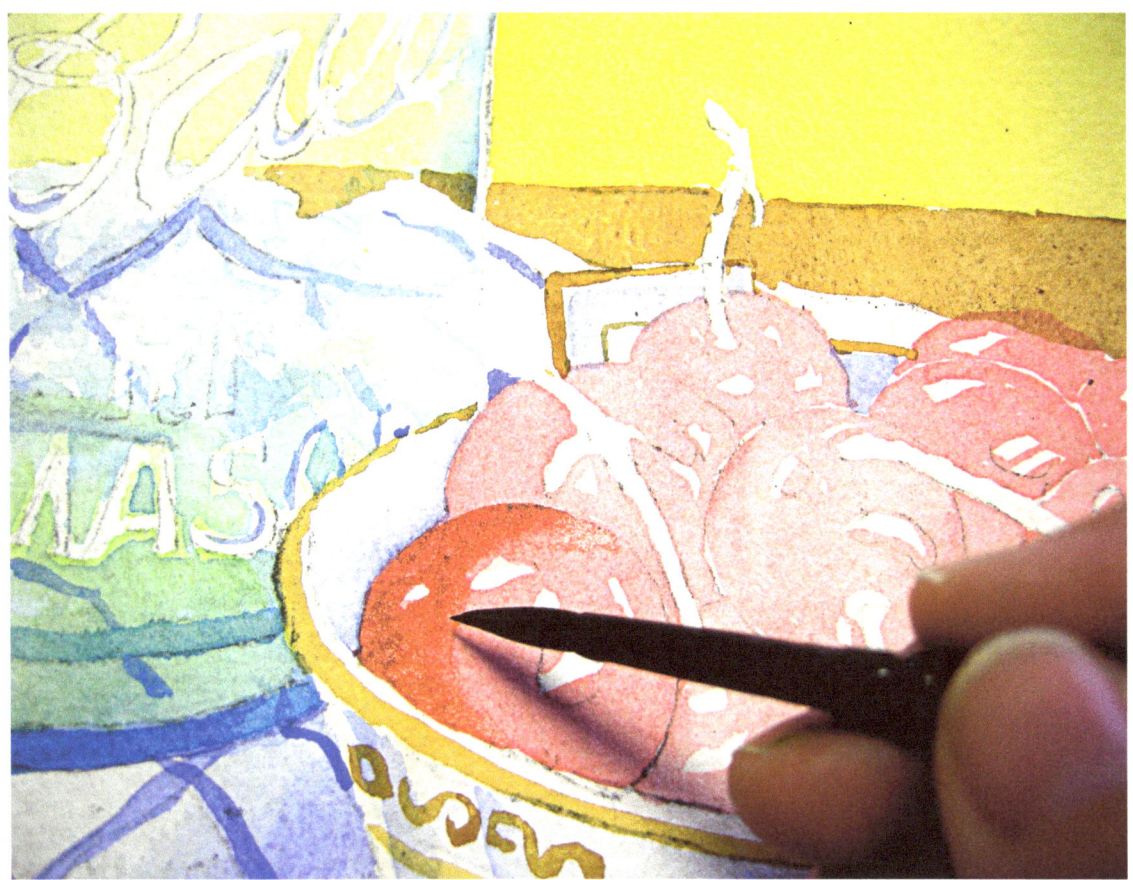

Back to painting the cherries! I wanted the cherries to look round, so I needed to focus on the values, shadows, and the direction the light is coming from. I also needed to be sure that I painted the shadow shapes correctly. Since we are creating the illusion of a three-dimensional subject on a two dimensional surface, the sure fire way to accomplish this is by correctly using color, value and shape.

Again, look at the reds on your palette. You may want to add some darker browns to your choices here, like VanDyke Brown. I started to use Permanent Alizarin Crimson to work in some of the shadow shapes around the cherries.

Be consistent with your light source. If the light is coming from the upper right, be sure the darkest shadows appear on the lower left. Some of the cherries will cast shadows here and there on the other objects.

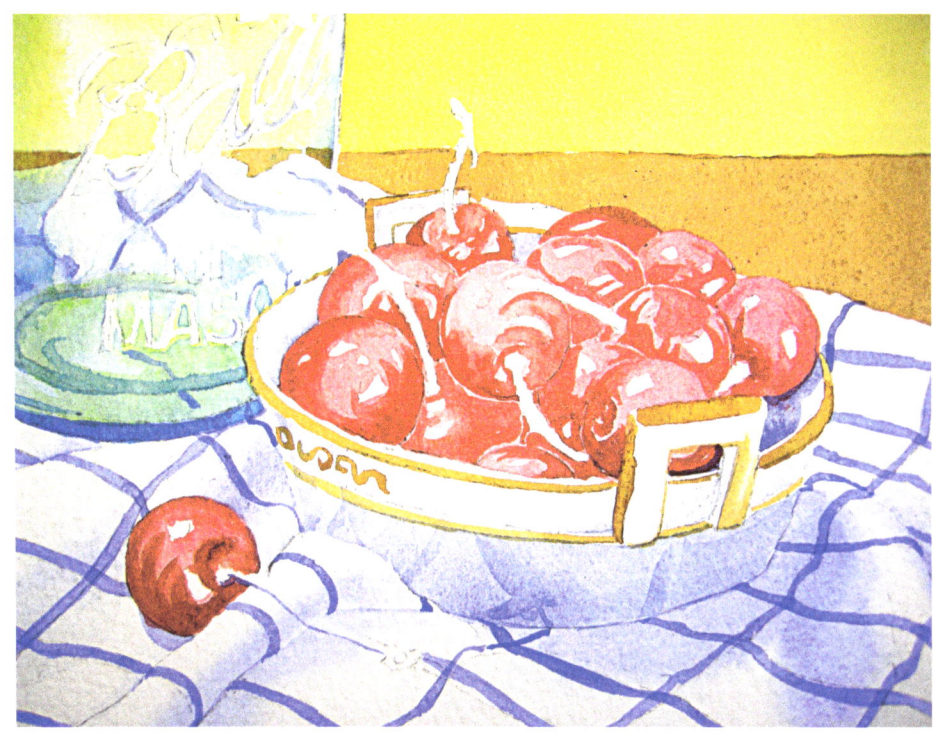

Quinacridone Gold and Burnt Sienna are the colors of the day! I used them to add some gold cast to the glass jar, especially at the bottom where the colors are darker because of the way the light hits the objects. I used a touch of this color at the top of the jar lid also. Notice the soft edges inside the jar.

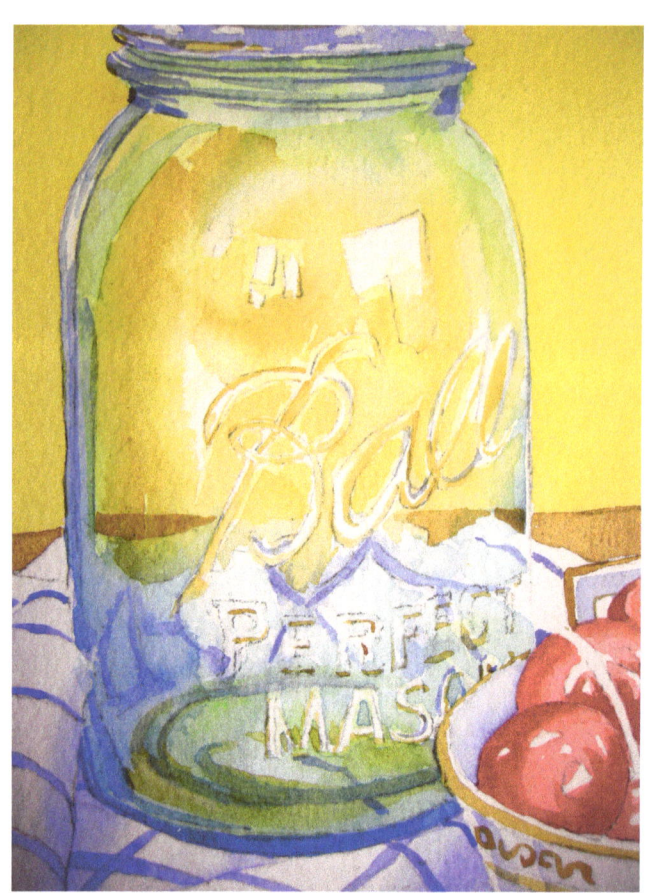

Some areas of glass will have crisp lines where the shadows are deep, like at the edge of a shape in the glass (notice the letters). Other crisp edges of color can be found where the light hits the glass directly. All of the other areas will have soft transitions of color by using clear water. Wet edges are soft edges. Dry paper will create crisp edges.

As you look through glass, it will distort the values and shapes of objects behind and under the glass. Notice how the jar is a bit darker than the wall.

I have been saying "notice" a lot. Think about it this way: you should look 90 percent of the time and paint 10 percent of the time. The more you look, the more you will see accurately. Then you will be able to create the impression of something realistic.

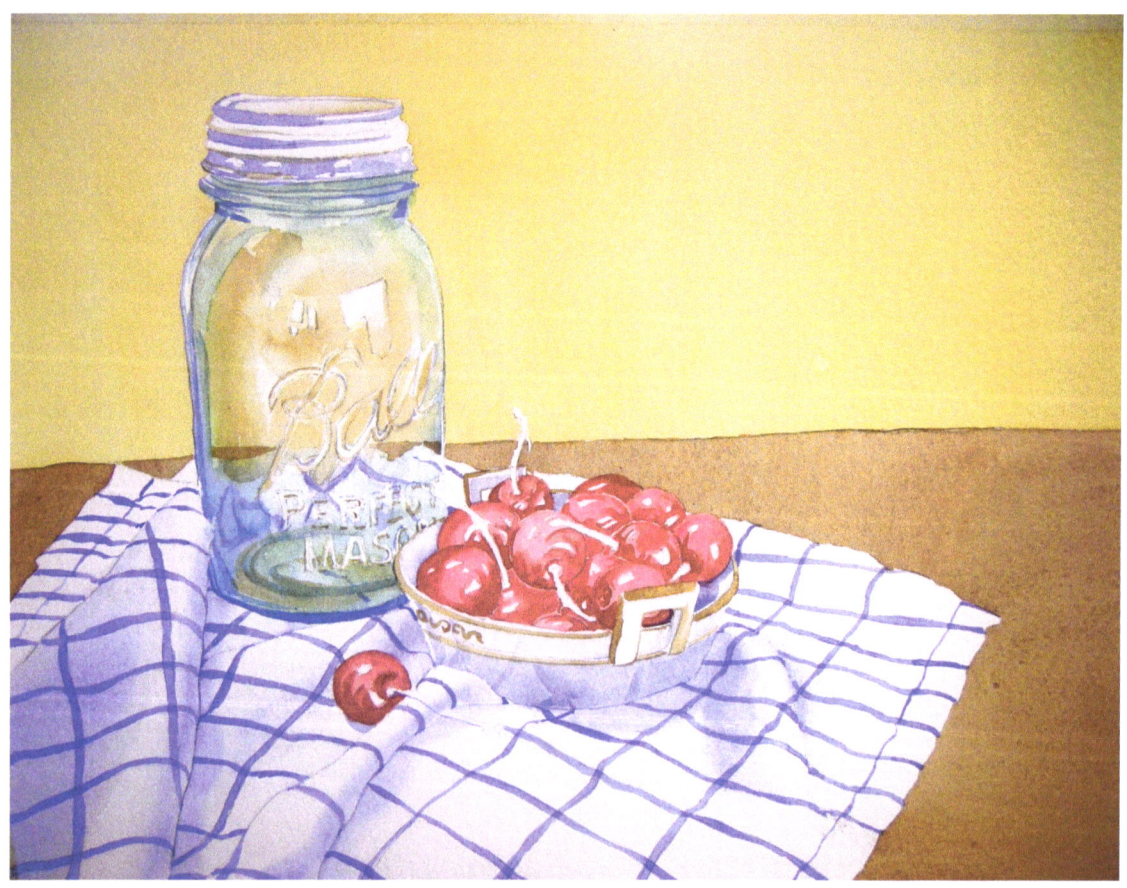

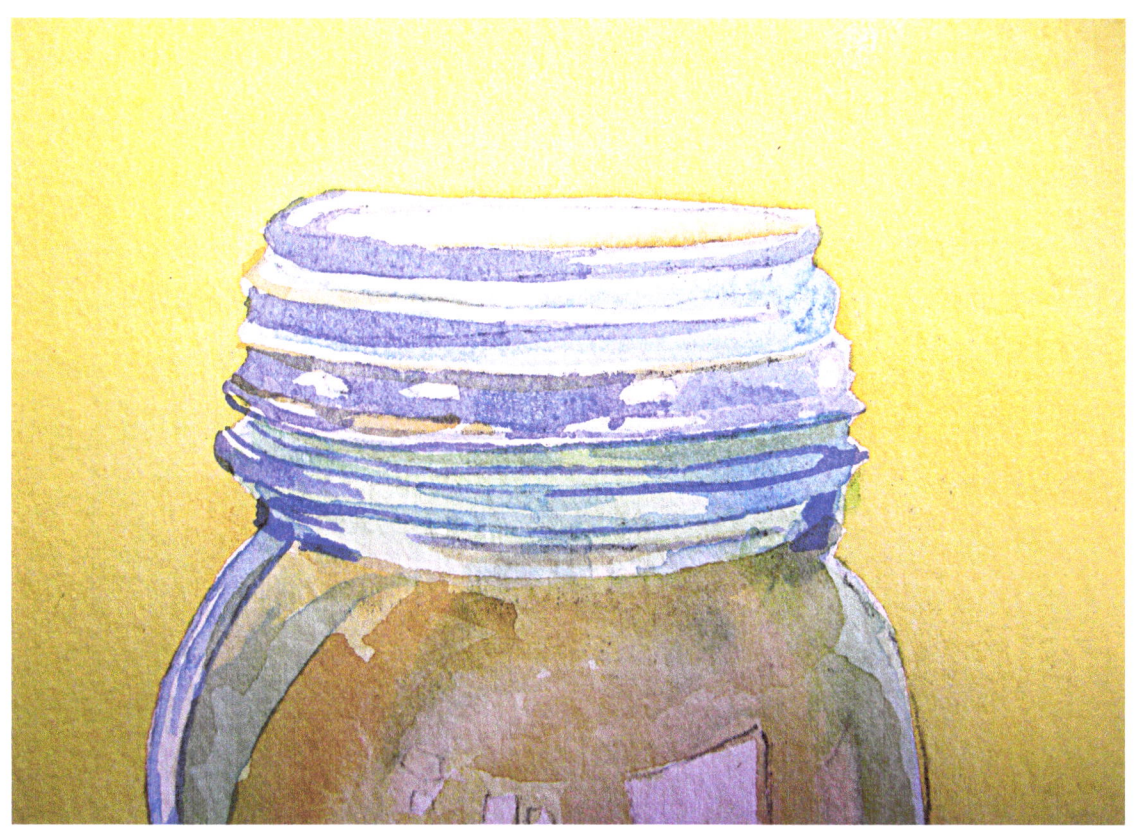

I used Prussian Blue to develop some of the shapes on the jar lid. Again shape is very important. Each line of pigment you paint should be done thoughtfully. I painted the shadows, not the raised, lighted areas. I painted around the light areas.

I used Prussian Blue to develop some more shadows in the jar also. I used it around the bottom of the lid, along the left edge, around the darkest shadows in the lettering, and at the bottom of the jar. It is really beginning to take shape!

I used a variety of reds from my palette to develop more depth in the cherries. I primarily used Permanent Alizarin Crimson, Perylene Maroon, and Winsor Red. I like to use these colors because they are transparent so when I glaze with them the colors underneath will show through. This makes the colors vibrant and rich.

I added some Permanent Sap Green and Burnt Sienna to the stems on the cherries.

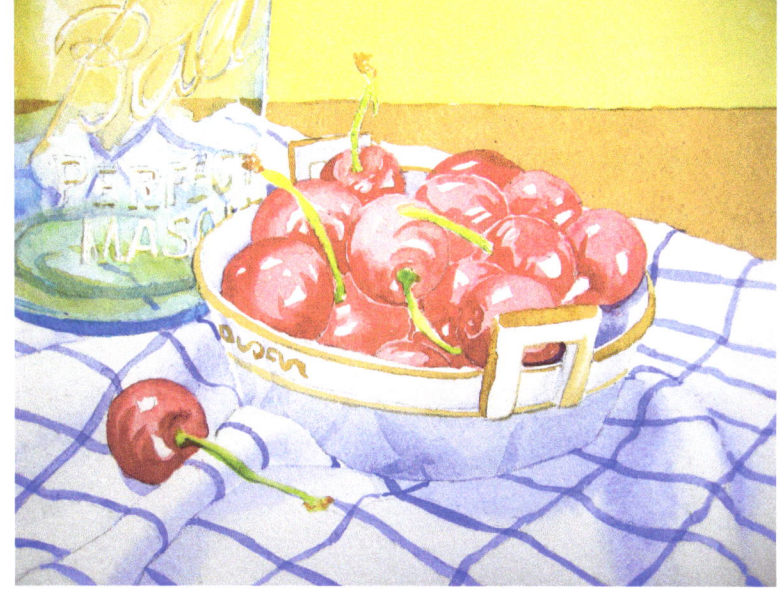

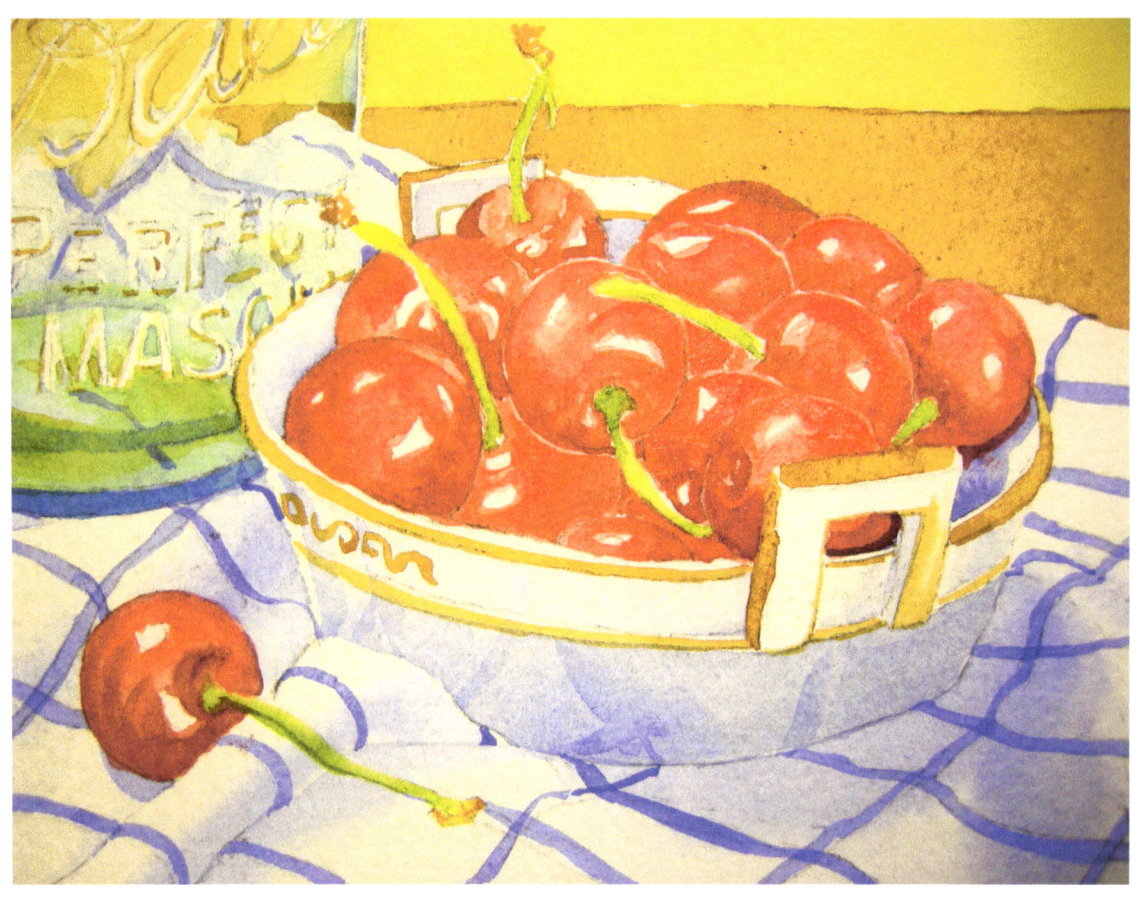

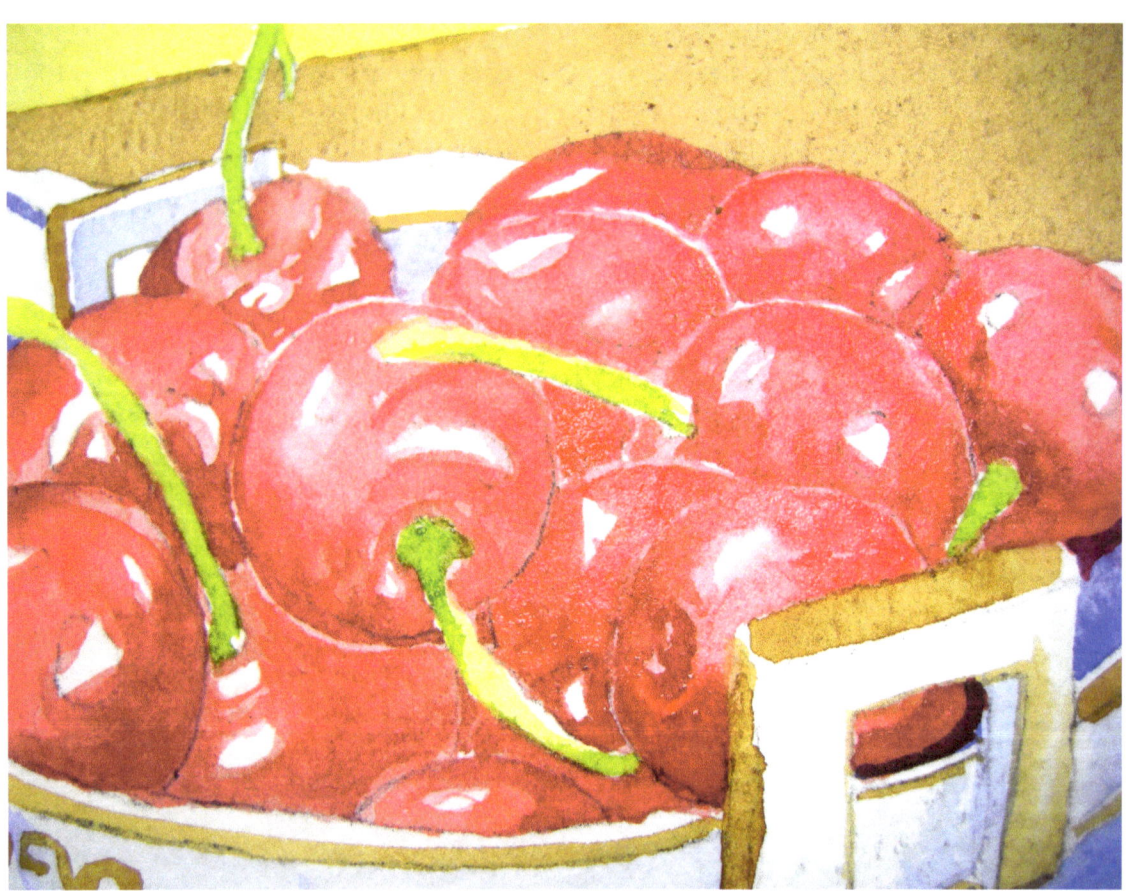

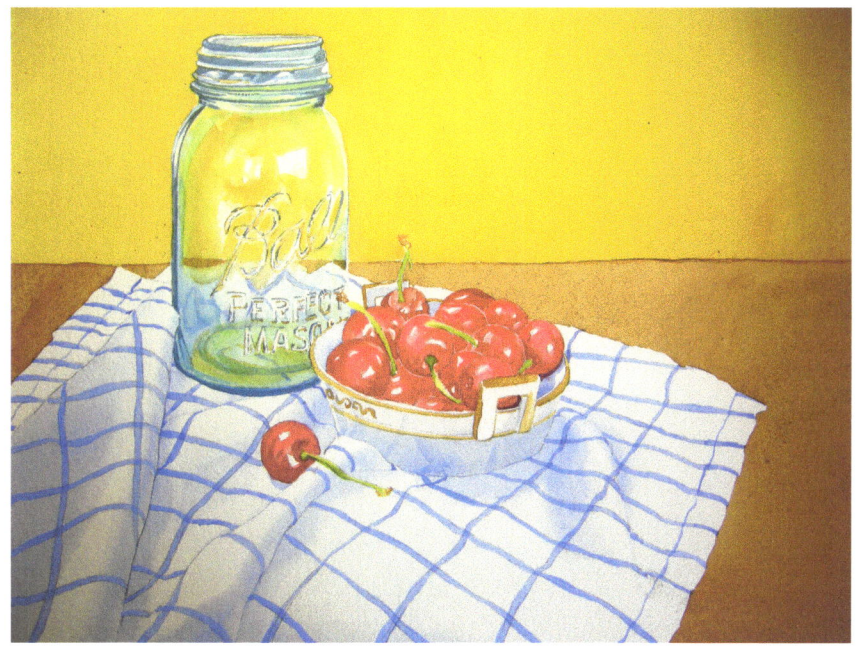

It is important to periodically take time to step back and take a good look at your painting. I wanted to be sure I was not overworking some areas. I like to keep the painting at the same stage of development throughout the entire process.

I like to write notes to myself of what I want to work on next. I check shapes, values, colors, and edges. I try to view the painting from a distance and from a few different angles to get a better perspective. Sometimes I hold it up in a mirror to see it from a more objective point of view.

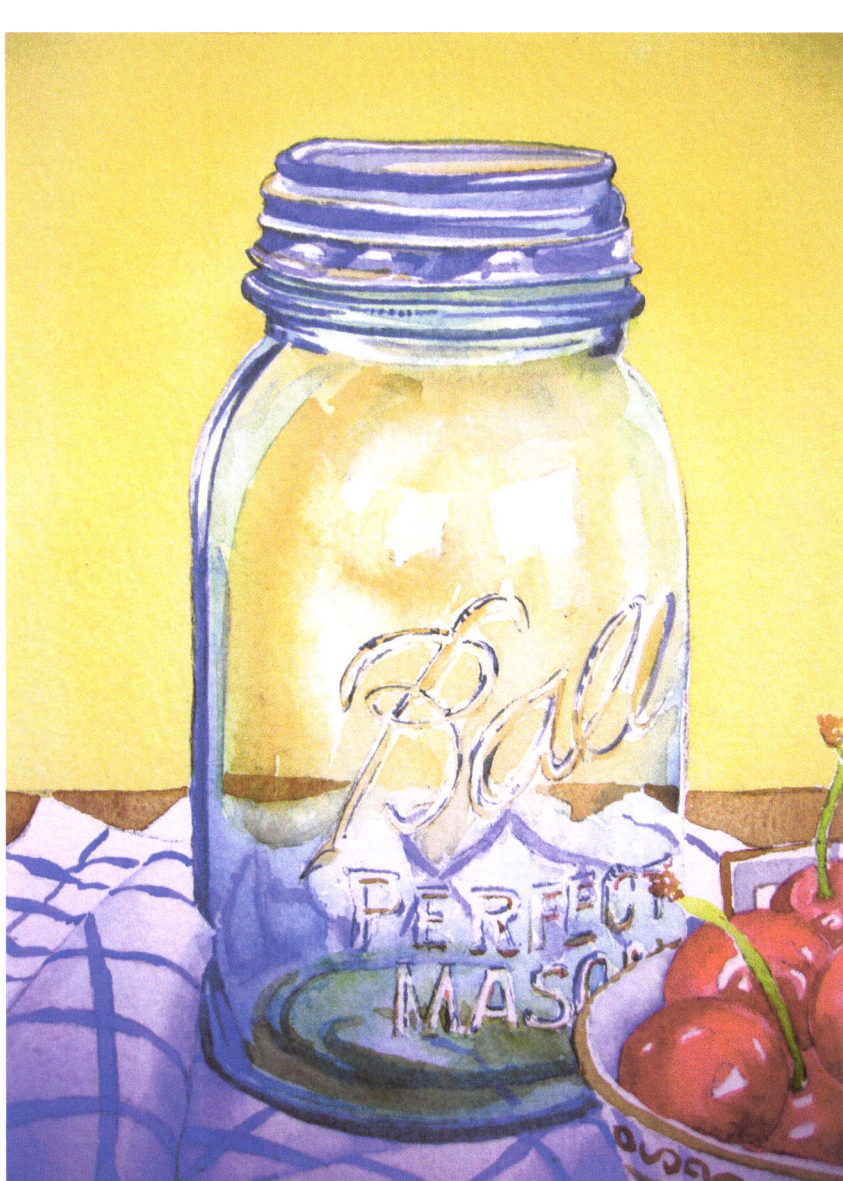

As I studied this piece I could see that I could add some darker values to the jar. I painted some of the warm colors used earlier in to the details of the lettering on the jar, saving the whites for where the light hit it directly. I added some Prussian Blue to some of the darker shadow areas around the piece, including the bottom edge of the white dish.

When I stepped back and looked at my progress, I noticed that the shadows in the towel were pretty cool. I wanted to warm them up a little!

I used a very wet wash of Burnt Sienna and glazed it over some (not all) of the shadow areas in the towel. This very light, wet wash, like a tea stain, helps to subtly warm up the shadows and make them look more natural.

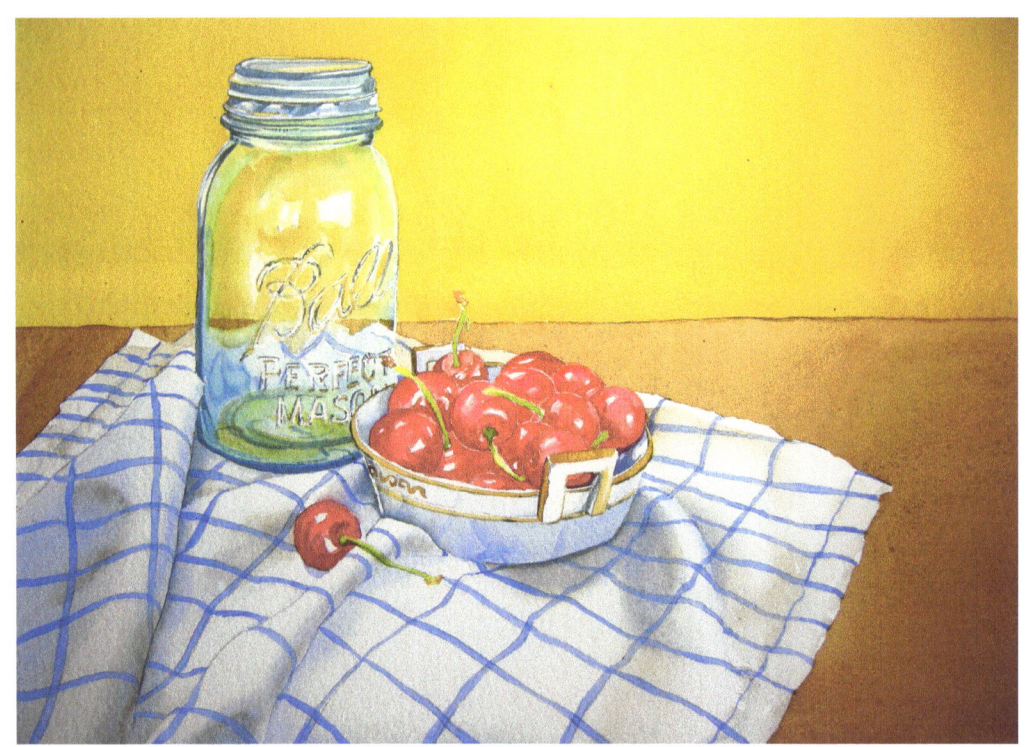

I added a touch of this color to the left side of the glass dish also, to help define the shape and shadows, and to add a tiny bit of reflection where the cherry on the table is shining into the side of the dish.

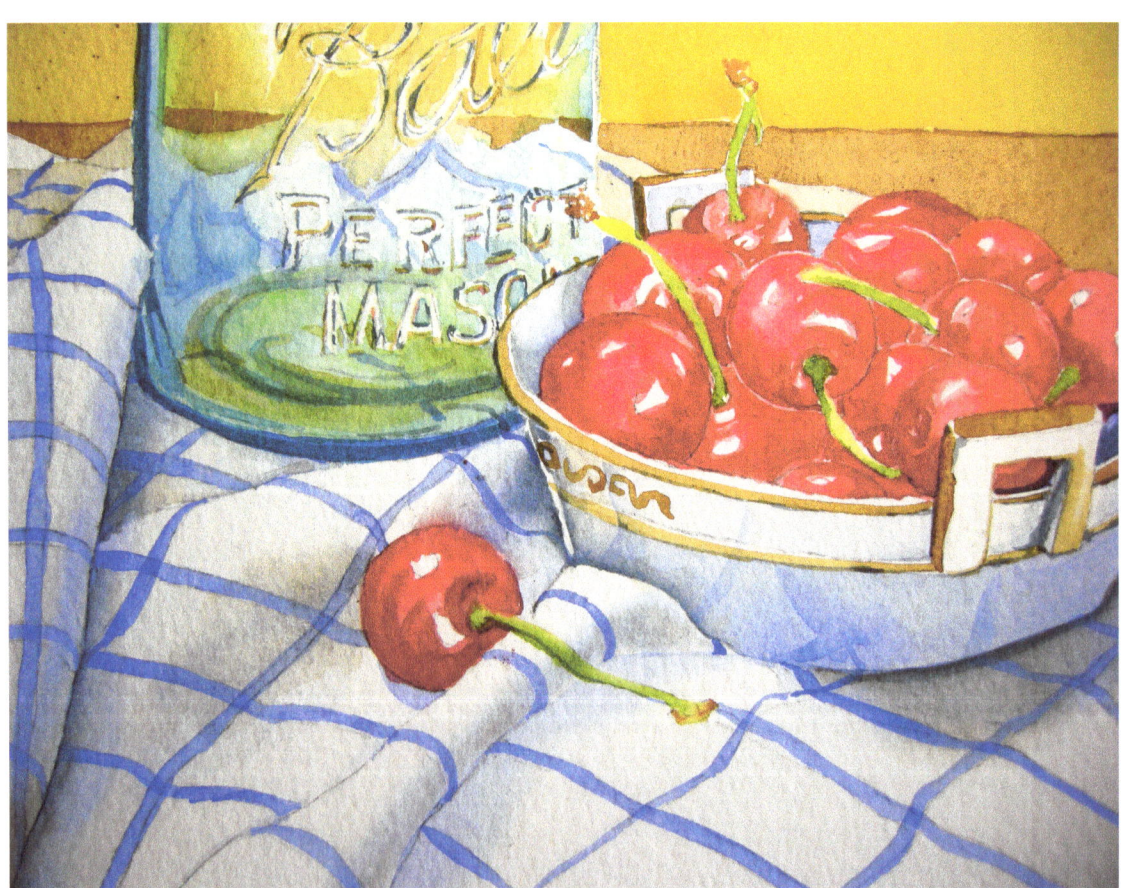

26

Now for some drama on the table.

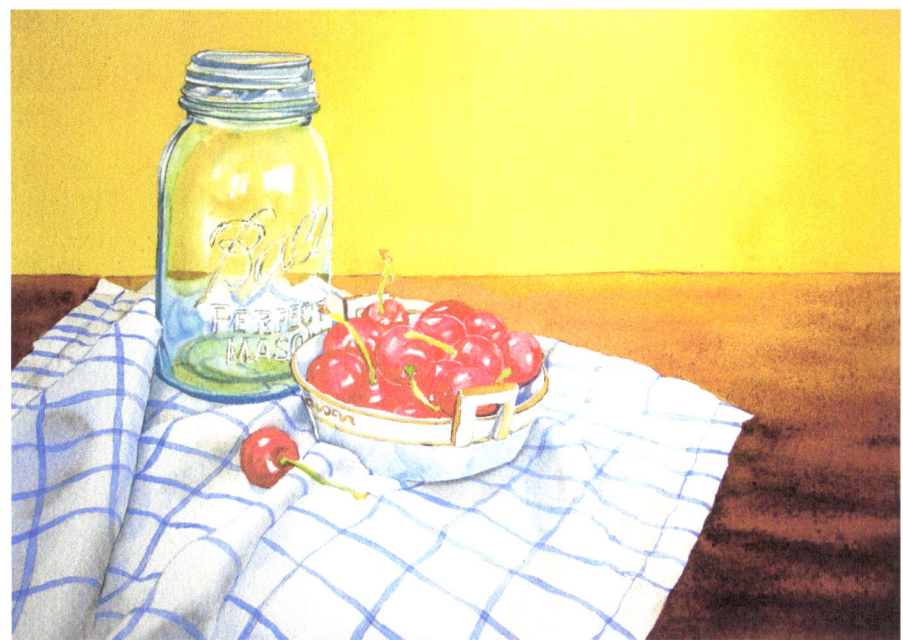

I mixed some Burnt Sienna and Van Dyke Brown to create a wash for the lower right corner of the table. I wanted to give it some weight, a darker value and a subtle texture like wood. First I glazed a little bit of water over the wood table area. I wanted to make the paper damp, not puddled.

Then I used horizontal strokes of strong color and laid on some texture. The wetness of the paper helps to soften the edges. I also tried to make the strokes non-uniform and darker on the bottom right than on the upper edge. This helped to create the illusion of depth.

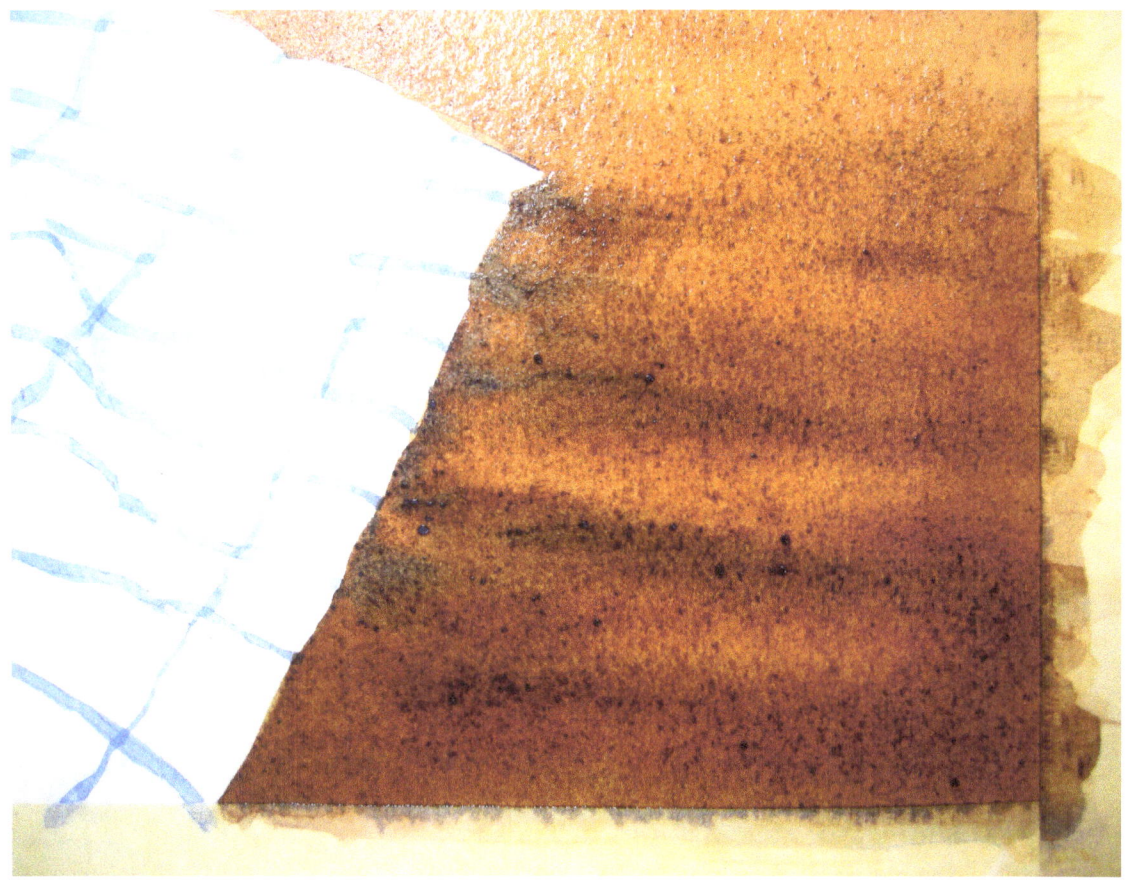

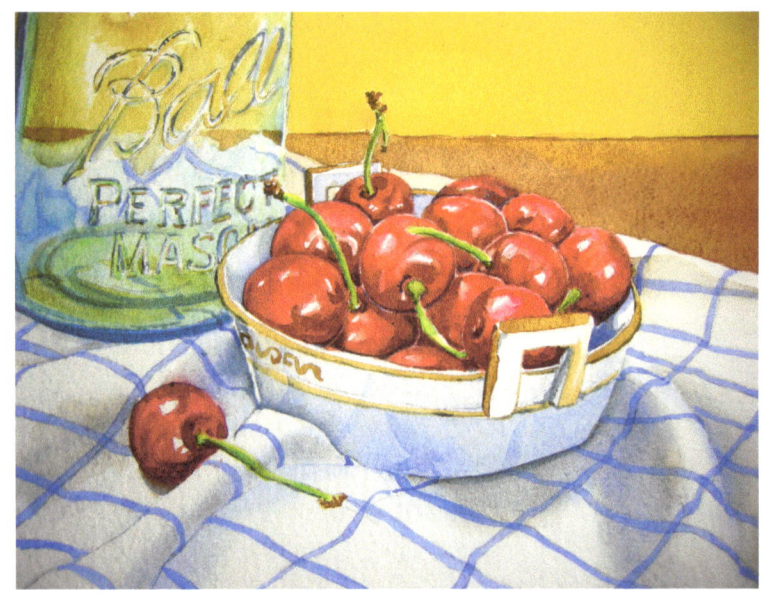

I used Van Dyke Brown and Perylene Maroon to add some very dark details to the cherry shadows. I used the Van Dyke Brown, fairly wet, to run tiny shadows along some of the stem areas. Avoid using this color along the entire edge or your edges may look to much like an illustration rather than a painting.

Move your piece to another room or in different light. Step back from the painting so you can see it from a different perspective. Hold it up to a mirror. Note anything that you may want to change and let it sit for a while. After some time, go back and make the changes. This is an important time to remember not to overwork your piece. I was once told, if you think you are almost done – stop!

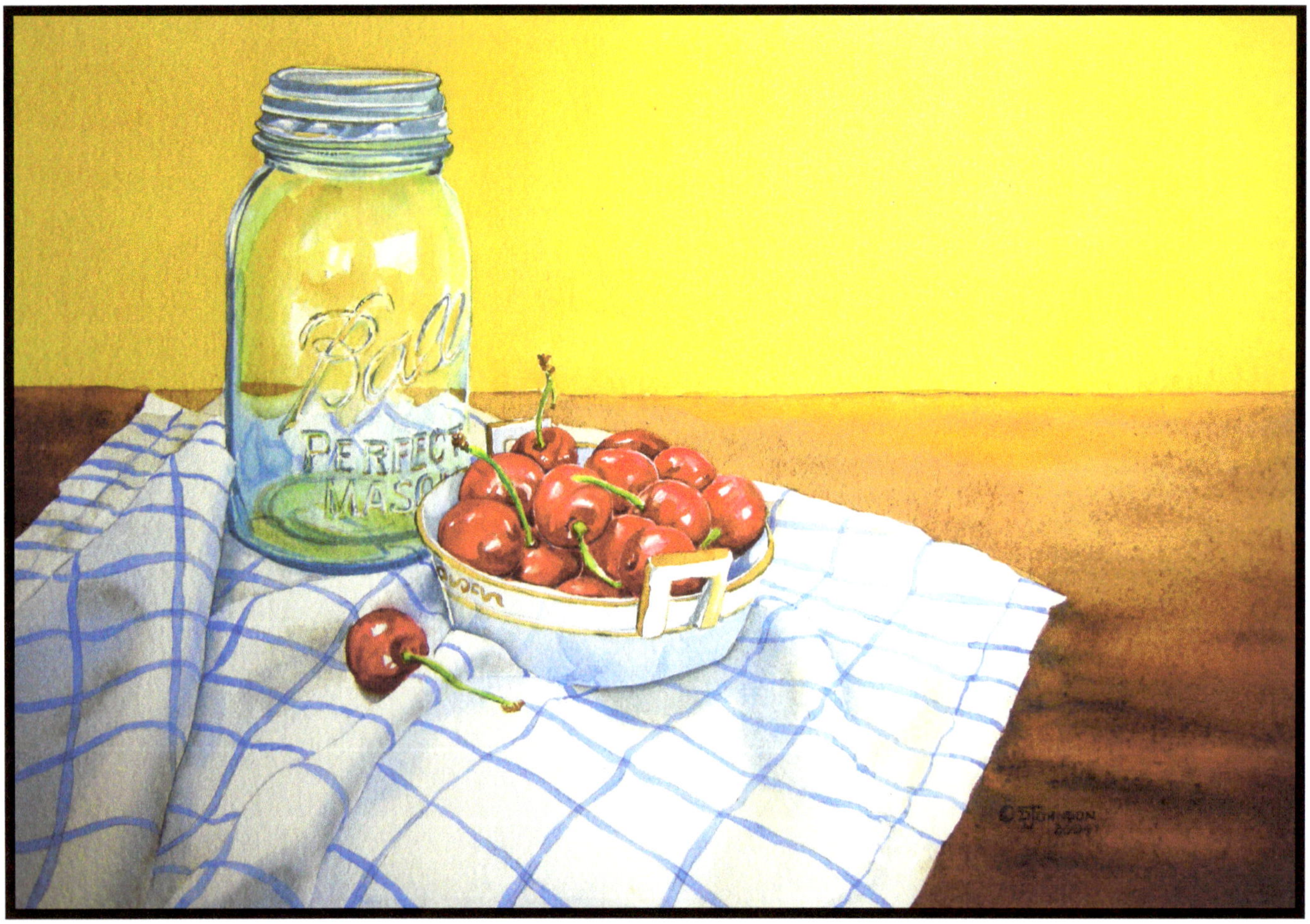

The finished piece! Once I sign a piece I don't allow myself to touch it with a brush again.

Reference Photos

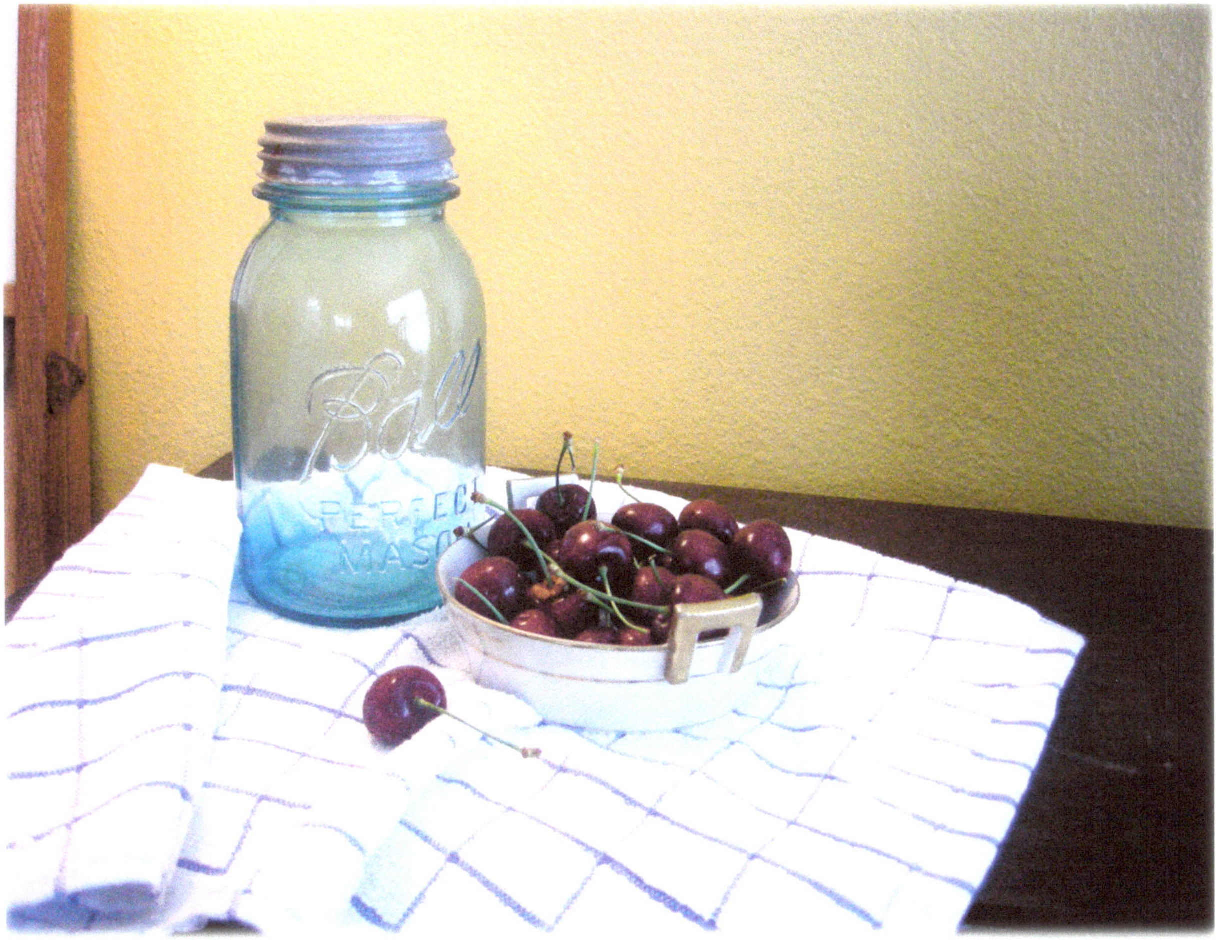

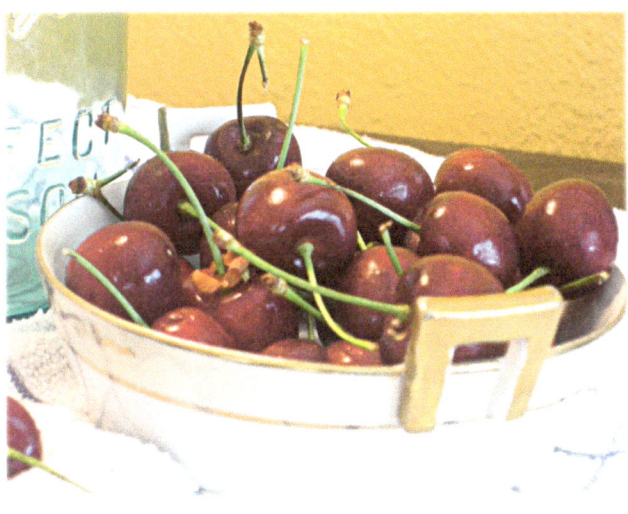

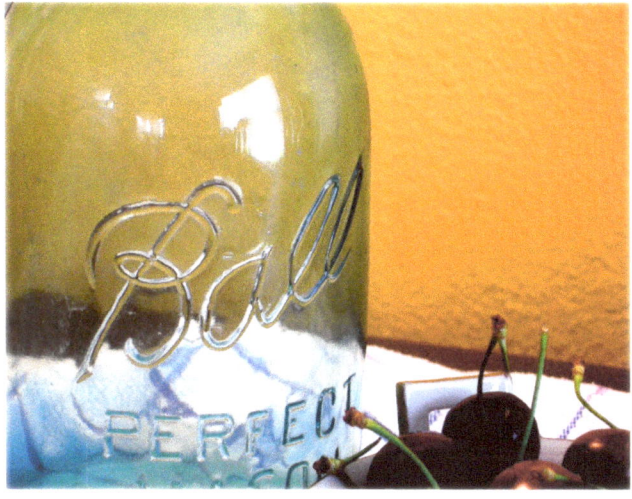

Removing the color from the reference photo helps me to see the values, the lights and darks, in the photo which give the two dimensional surface of the photo an illusion of space and shape.

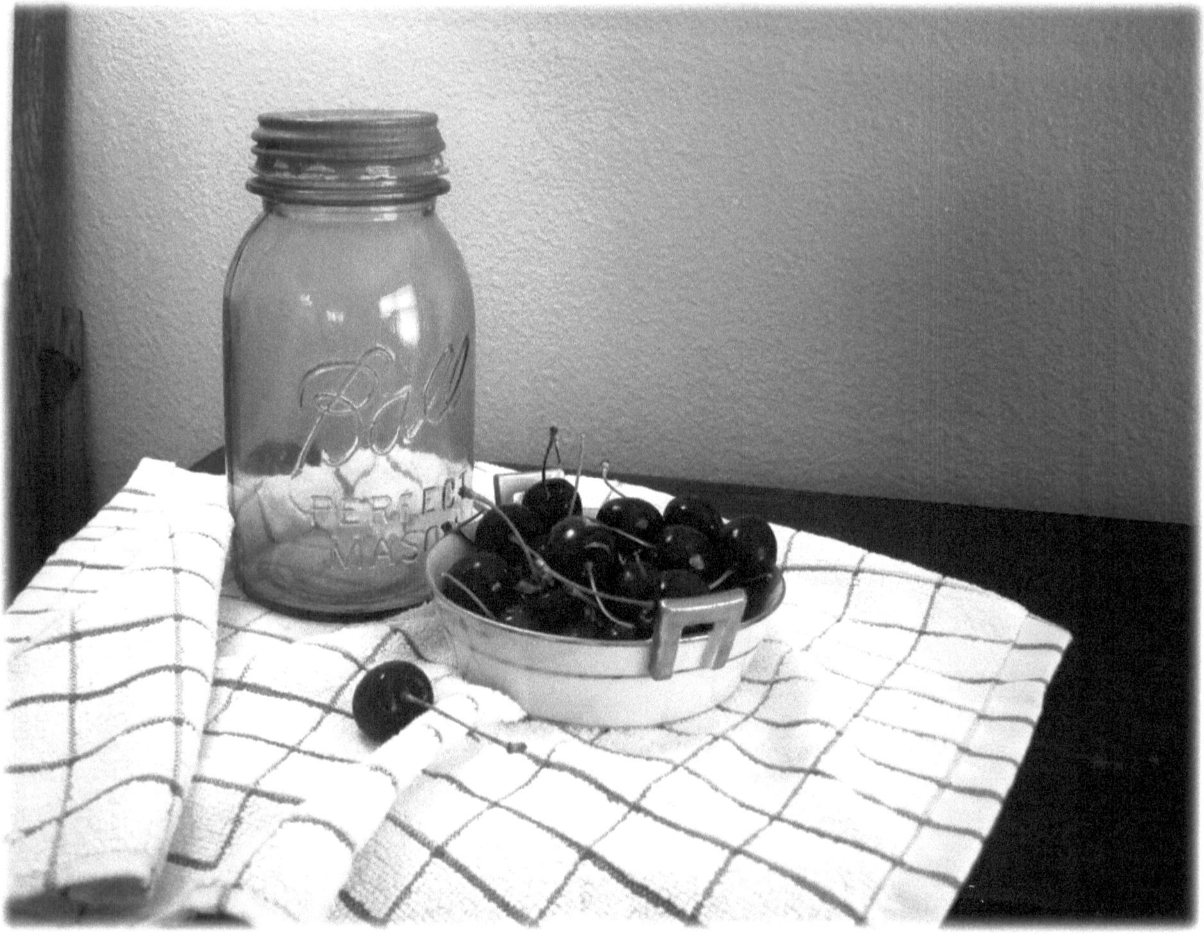

Look at the value chart below and try to see where those values are represented in the grayscale photo reference.

Value Chart

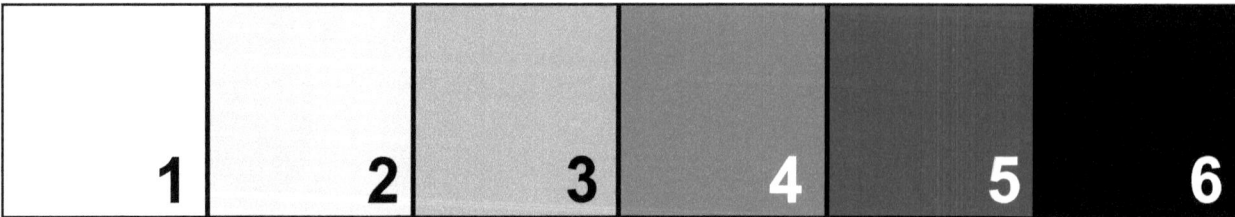

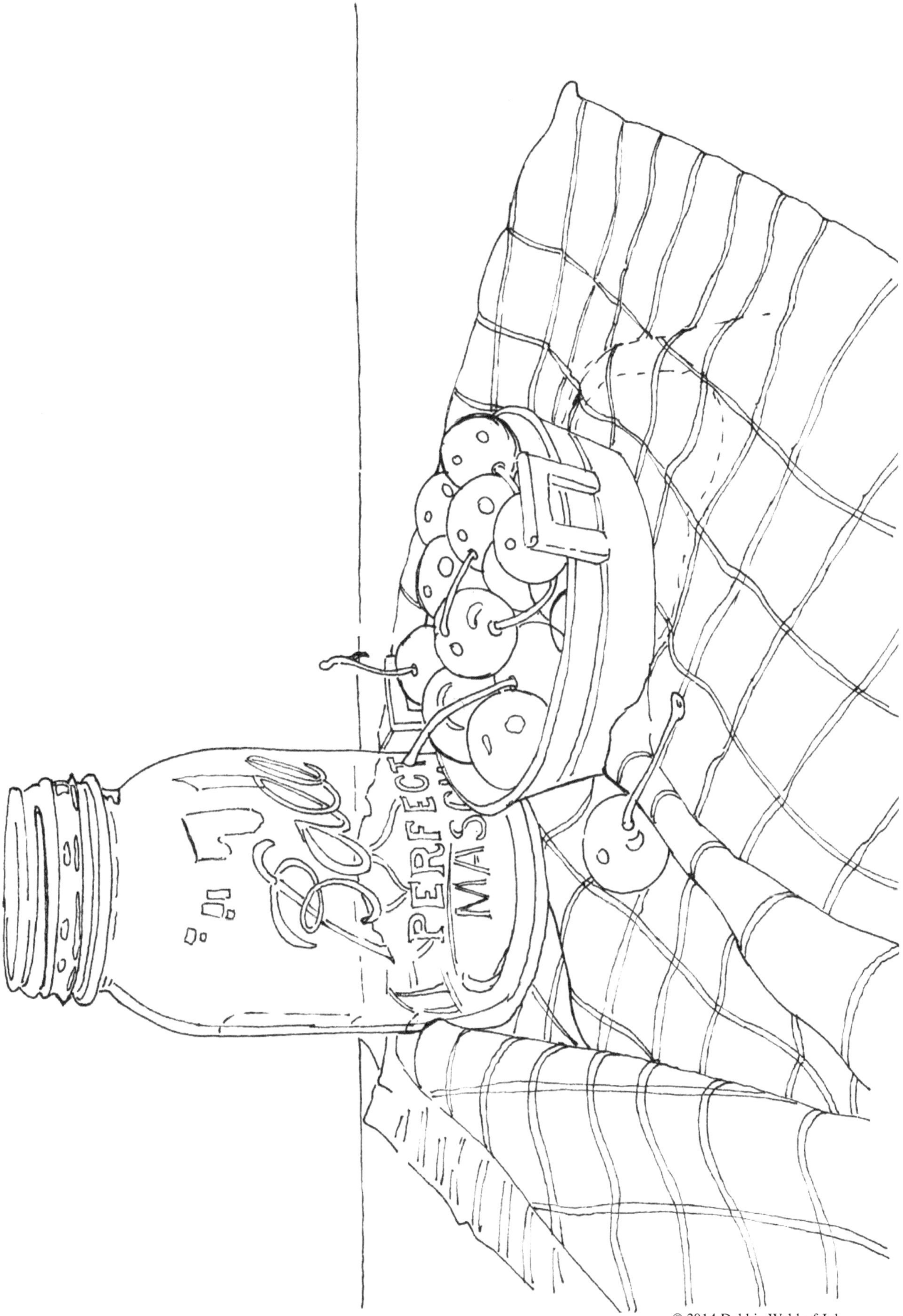

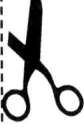

This drawing can be traced onto watercolor paper for practice.
This page may be copied or enlarged for your personal use only.

Suggested Watercolor Supplies

- 11" x 14" pad of Arches 140 lb. watercolor paper, or larger
- 1" Flat brush, natural hair, or natural hair/synthetic blend
- No. 10 round brush, natural hair or natural hair/synthetic blend
- No. 6 round brush, natural hair or natural hair/synthetic blend
- Palette with large mixing wells and 1" or wider paint wells
  My favorite palette is CheapJoes Piggy Back.
- Windsor Newton (Professional Grade/not student grade) Pigments: Aureolin Yellow, New Gamboge, Winsor Red, Permanent Alizarin Crimson, Burnt Sienna, Raw Umber, VanDyke Brown, Perylene Maroon, Hookers Green, Cerulean Blue, French Ultramarine Blue, Indigo. Any other colors you may like to use. Other good brands are: Maimeriblu, Holbein, and Daler-Rowney. Look for transparent colors.
- White Vinyl Eraser
- Sketchbook, any kind
- Large water container (1 lb. deli tub works great)
- Paper Towel
- No. 2 Pencil
- 2 inch Wide Masking Tape (Not blue painter's tape)
- Masking Fluid
- Masking Fluid Brush
- Masking Fluid Pickup Tool
- Two small containers for masking and soap.

Have fun experimenting with colors, brushes, and techniques. Every artist has their favorite tools and methods which is what makes them unique.

Great Online Art Supply Resources:

www.cheapjoes.com
jerrysartarama.com
www.dickblick.com
www.aswexpress.com
www.utrechtart.com
www.artsuppliesonline.com

Be sure to check with your local art supply store first.

Debbie Waldorf Johnson has more lessons on her website:
http://debbiejohnsonartist.wordpress.com/Lessons
You will find step-by-step lessons in blog format as well as links to videos of how to correctly develop watercolor washes.